A GUIDE TO PRACTICAL PASTORING

A Guide to Practical Pastoring

BARNEY COOMBS

KINGSWAY PUBLICATIONS
EASTBOURNE

ISBN 0 85476 380 5

Produced by Bookprint Creative Services
P.O. Box 827, BN23 6NX, England for
KINGSWAY PUBLICATIONS LTD
Lottbridge Drove, Eastbourne, E Sussex BN23 6NT.
Printed in England by Clays Ltd, St Ives plc

Contents

Foreword 7
Preface 9
Acknowledgements 11

PART ONE: HEART AND SOUL ISSUES 13
1. Managers or Leaders 14
2. Square Peg in a Round Hole 20
3. Square-peg Symptoms 26
4. Discovering Your Gift 39
5. He Who Serves, Leads 44
6. Owners or Stewards 50
7. The Doughnut-hole Principle 54
8. Take Care How You Build 64
9. Not Many Fathers 71
10. Grace Is Free but Not Cheap 78
11. The Leader's Authority 89

PART TWO: PRACTICAL ISSUES 99
12. Bereavement and Funerals 100
13. Preparing a Couple for Marriage 110
14. The Wedding 122
15. Baptisms 127
16. Cells for Life 133
17. Cells for Growth 146
18. Teaching the Scriptures 159
19. Murphy Versus O'Shaunessy: When Calamity Strikes 174
20. Things to Do or Not to Do 180

Epilogue 192

To the memory of my dear father Sidney Coombs who taught me by word and deed that the only thing that really mattered in life was to live for Christ.

And to my dear mother Kathleen Coombs who taught me by her godly example that the only way to live for Christ was to give until there was nothing else left to give.

Foreword

There is a great need in the church for books by practitioners. This is such a book.

Principles are vital if we are to be effective in the long run. This is as true of an individual as it is of a church. Individually and corporately there are principles that will keep us sharp, influential and effective for the gospel.

Motivation is of prime importance if we are to sustain a good start. But a practical approach will save us from being simply highly motivated and principled, yet strangely ineffective.

The difference between aspiration and achievement is development. Charismatic churches, even new churches (house churches), can be immensely insensitive, impractical, and in the name of spirituality leave common sense in the garage, garden shed or the kitchen. It is difficult to develop something that has been left behind!

What is so good about Barney Coombs' publication is the ability to twin good principles with good practice. This in itself provides a high level of motivation with high principles.

Primarily Barney Coombs is a people person. I've seen him as an evangelist, church planter and a leader amongst leaders. But it is his ability to understand people, get under their skin and make them feel wanted and valued, that creates the loyalty in his network of relationships and is the strength of this book. Complete strangers—'nobodies'—come into view in several chapters, and we see that these people matter to Barney; this is where he models something to his readers.

The practical aspect of the book develops as Barney has clearly seen many new church leaders struggling or ill at ease conducting weddings, funerals and a host of other events. I am glad he has written about these apparently mundane issues in such an unembarrassing, matter-of-fact way. It is worth re-emphasising that this is not rehashing someone else's ideas; it comes out of many years of actually learning the best way of doing things.

I am totally against taking people out of local church situations to put them into academic, ivory towers, returning students as unskilled in pastoral and practical issues as when they started.

Doing it is doing it. But I am for learning on the job, learning from others and benefiting from father-figures who actually care about how things are done, why they are done and who they are done for.

I pray that this publication will develop aspirations into achievements through a highly motivated, practical outworking of the principles God has given us. This is not simply something to live for, but the stuff through which God's kingdom will be extended.

When you have read this book make sure your up-and-coming leaders see it soon.

Gerald Coates

Preface

Over the last twenty-five years there has been a proliferation of leaders among what has become known as the 'new churches'. The church, in general, has welcomed with open arms the concept of meeting in small groups; thus the need for new leaders.

These new leaders increasingly are taking over many of the activities that used to belong exclusively to the professional clergy, such as weddings, funerals, hospital visitation and counselling. However, almost all of these leaders have had no formal pastoral training whatsoever. The situation has recently become even more interesting in that some people who used to lead a house church of about 20 folk now pastor congregations of 500 or more.

The following chapters are designed to help leaders avoid making unnecessary errors as they pastor God's flock. This is not intended to be an exhaustive treatise on pastoral care in the house church movement, but rather, it is meant to give a few pointers that might be of service to the budding leader.

Much of what I have learned has come through mistakes made out of ignorance, mostly of my own making, but sometimes I have been instructed through the errors of others. 'Wisdom cries aloud on every street corner.'

I have deliberately used many anecdotes. This is

designed to keep the reader awake while the mind is hopefully being penetrated with helpful thoughts or suggestions. 'A spoonful of sugar helps the medicine go down!' Besides, God made sure the Scriptures were saturated with interesting stories. I don't think I can improve on his style, but how I wish I knew and understood more of his ways!

Barney Coombs

Acknowledgements

My dear friends David and Rosemary Freeman have been of inestimable help in editing the entire manuscript. They were ably supported by Mary MacLean and David Richards. Writing a book is not easy for me. My use of the English language leaves much to be desired; how I wish I had been more attentive at school! As a result, numerous changes have been made. The blessing of giving the credit to these kind people is that now, if the reader finds any errors, it is they who will get the blame!

My sincere thanks goes also to Barbara Gyde, Daniella Ross, Ann Murgatroyd and Vicki Elgar who all patiently endeavoured to decipher my writing before committing it to the computer, and to Chris Auber together with Adam Pink who painstakingly transferred the manuscript from one computer system to another.

I am particularly grateful to Steven May-Miller for baring his soul in Chapter 3. Many people who have passed through similar struggles will find his experience enlightening.

To all those who have graciously allowed me to practise at being their pastor—who not only witnessed my mistakes, but sometimes were at the receiving end—thank you with all my heart. Whatever there is of worth and substance in me today is due in part to your patience, forgiveness and understanding.

I constantly thank the Lord for my wife and children. Janette and I have been married for thirty-four years. Apart from the Lord's sovereign grace, her love, support and prayers have been the most singular reason why I have survived thus far in the ministry. Stephen, together with his wife Janet, their two children Devon Anne and Leighton Barnabas; Mark and, Jacqueline, with their three children Jessica, Justine and Taylor; and Rachel who is married to Jeremy, and their little baby Estee Elizabeth have all in their own way added richness and colour to my role as a pastor.

Finally, but most importantly, I want to say how deeply moved I am that my heavenly Father, knowing the very worst about me, none the less called and set me apart to be a shepherd to his flock. I enjoyed the challenge and adventure of the Metropolitan Police but the past twenty-six years have been the most fulfilling years of my life. There is no greater honour than to serve the living God. Some people count it a great privilege to serve their monarch or president, but we are workers together with God. What a priceless privilege!

PART ONE

Heart and Soul Issues

I

Managers or Leaders

> We trained hard, but it seemed that every time we were beginning to form up in teams we would be reorganised. I was to learn later in life that we tend to meet any new situation by reorganising and a wonderful method it can be for creating the illusion of progress whilst producing confusion, inefficiency and demoralisation.
>
> Gaius Petronius (AD 66)

My first year as a pastor was unforgettable. At that time Basingstoke was still a small, English market town with a population of about 19,000.

One incident still stands out clearly in my memory. I was watching the local soccer team play Waterlooville in a preliminary round of the FA Cup. Basingstoke were losing in spite of an all-out effort and a small section of the crowd began to barrack them. One man standing near to me was particularly vociferous in his disapproval. Finally, the right back for Basingstoke could stand it no longer; coming over to where we were standing he offered to give his boots to anyone who thought they could do better. Seeing no one who would take his place, he rejoined the game. I recall thinking to myself, 'That typifies this town: quick to criticise, slow to applaud.'

Shortly after this I attended a Fountain Trust conference at High Leigh, Hoddesdon, just north of London.

Among the many speakers was Arthur Wallis, one of the founding fathers of the charismatic renewal movement. One night during the conference I had a most disturbing experience. It can only be described as something between a dream and a nightmare. I was walking down a country lane with fields either side at eye level. Steep banks topped with a barbed wire fence kept cattle in and discouraged would-be trespassers. Suddenly my attention was seized by the appearance of a wild, ferocious-looking animal, half cat and half wolf. I was horrified to see a petite, bambi-like creature in its jaws, its beady mouse-like eyes filled with fear. The beast dumped the little deer down on the ground, still holding it with its sharp, pointed fangs. I can still vividly recall its tiny hoofs hitting the ground. Its fate was sealed unless someone came to the rescue. Without thinking, I clambered up the embankment and reached through the fence, being careful to maintain a safe position. But before I could get anywhere near it, the beast drew back on its hind legs, its teeth digging deep into the delicate furry skin as it gripped the poor little animal more firmly. Simultaneously, a blood vessel shaped like a large boil slowly protruded out of the back of the little creature's head.

With this I woke up, sitting bolt upright in bed, beads of perspiration covering my face. What was the meaning of this? Was this a satanic attack? Was God speaking to me? Deeply disturbed, I resolved to share it with Arthur Wallis the very next day.

All who knew Arthur were aware that here was a man of integrity who was seldom given to prayerless, quick replies and never to pat answers. He carefully listened to my story, but after praying with me he answered, 'Quite frankly Barney, the Lord isn't showing me anything. Let's just commit it all to him further and if there is anything significant he will reveal it in his good time.'

The conference turned out to be a crossroads that

would change the whole course of my life. Without question I encountered the Lord. It was clear my peacekeeping role was achieving precious little and, more importantly, God was not amused with my efforts. So before leaving High Leigh I entered into a covenant with the Lord that went like this: 'From now on, whatever he directed me to do, as best I knew how, I would be obedient, leaving the consequences with him.' I understood it would be one step at a time and that only after careful obedience would further revelation be forthcoming. In one dramatic conversion I changed from management to leadership.

As I look back on those early days, it is easy to see that I had been a manager. But from that conference onwards I became a leader.

Shepherds lead: 'He leads me beside quiet waters.... He guides me in the paths of righteousness' (Ps 23:2-3). 'He calls his own sheep by name, and leads them out. ...he goes before them, and the sheep follow him' (Jn 10:3-4). The absence of good, clear leadership is a number one problem worldwide. It is no less a problem within the church. It is not possible to keep everybody happy but it is possible to be a God-pleaser and lead God's people God's way with God's strength and wisdom.

Six months later I was visiting a farm in Hampshire with a good friend and happened to mention my dream-cum-nightmare. He later shared my dream with a close friend of his whom God uses uniquely in interpretation of dreams. He was careful not to give a hint of who I was or what I was involved in. Not long after, I received this reply with the interpretation: 'This brother is an elevated position within an organisation. (How accurate he was, we certainly were more of an organisation than a committed, related family of God.) In the organisation there are two extremes who are in contention with each other, typified in the half-cat half-wolf beast. The bambi-like creature represents a group of new babies in Christ also within this organisation. The life of the flesh is in the blood and the very life is being squeezed out of these new Christians, seen in the blood vessel rising out of the head. The brother has to get over the fence and into the situation if he wants to rescue the young believers. This dream is mostly in retrospect (meaning that I had indeed got over the fence), but tell the brother he will yet have to contend with both extremes.'

How accurate that interpretation proved to be! I was on one occasion watching '60 Minutes Live'—a USA television current affairs programme. The oldest serving officer in the American armed forces was about to retire. The officer was a seventy year old lady in charge of training computer operators for the Navy. The interviewer asked the question, 'Is there much difference between America today and when you were a young girl?'

'Oh yes,' she readily replied, 'We have become a nation of managers. We don't have many leaders.' She continued, 'My father used to say you manage things but you lead people.' God used this lady to write a truth upon my heart that will never be erased.

Leaders are those who are convinced God has called them and set them apart. This is absolutely fundamental; for without this understanding we can be assured we will behave like managers. To be a leader we need a distinct God-inspired vision. Without a vision there's nowhere to go; if we aim at nothing we are sure to hit it. Dr David Cormack describes the problem in his book *Seconds Away* (Marc Europe) as 'the ring of despair'. He puts it this way: without vision there is no direction, without direction there is no purpose, without purpose there are no targets, without targets there are no priorities, without priorities there is no plan and without a plan there is no hope.

A leader is one who not only sees the vision clearly but is able to communicate it to others in a manner that is easily understood, and with a passion that excites people enough to want to buy into it. A leader is one who is out in front leading by example, unlike Alexandre Auguste

Ledru-Rollin, a French lawyer and left wing revolutionary leader of the working class in the revolt 1830-1840, who was once heard to remark 'Ah well! I am their leader, I really ought to follow them!' A leader is one who is willing to take risks; not foolish irresponsible risks, but the sort of necessary steps the Bible calls faith.

Management is a nice, unchallenging, uneventful, safe place to be, but how boring, how soul-destroying, how disheartening to would-be martyrs! It reminds me of a poem I once heard:

> I think my soul is a tame old duck
> Dibbling round in farmyard muck,
> Fat and lazy with useless wings.
> But sometimes when the north wind sings
> And wild ducks hurtle overhead
> It remembers something lost and dead
> And cocks a wary puzzled eye
> And makes a feeble attempt to fly.
> It's fairly content with the state it's in
> But I think of the duck it might have been.

No! To be a true leader means comfort zones are disturbed—blood, sweat and tears are the order of the day. Just when everybody is nicely settled and all the tents are perfectly in order the cloud moves on. It is a life of risk, yes! and sometimes mistakes. But God would rather have a 'Peter' with his foot-shaped mouth and his irrepressible impetuosity than the man who, for reasons of self-preservation, buried his talent in the ground. Those famous lines from President Theodore Roosevelt sum it up perfectly:

> It is not the critic who counts: not the man who points out how the strong man stumbled or where the doer of deeds could have done them better. The credit belongs to the man who is actually in the arena; whose face is marred by dust and sweat and blood; who strives valiantly; who errs, and comes short again and again, because there is no effort without error

and shortcoming; who does actually try to do the deed; who knows the great enthusiasm, the great devotion and spends himself in a worthy cause; who, at the worst, if he fails, at least fails while daring greatly.

Far better it is to dare mighty things, to win glorious triumphs even though checkered by failure, than to rank with those poor spirits who neither enjoy nor suffer much because they live in the grey twilight that knows neither victory nor defeat.

2

Square Peg in a Round Hole

Janette and I, with our three young children, were taking our first vacation since I had become the pastor of Basingstoke Baptist Church. Whom to leave in charge was a real concern. I chose Brian (not his real name), one of the deacons who was a particularly good Bible teacher.

Brian was an excellent husband with a warm, loving wife and family to match. He was highly esteemed in his job, with a fine Christian reputation. On the basis of the required qualifications for an elder in 1 Timothy 3 he passed with flying colours. A consistent, trustworthy, godly man, I was certain that not only would the church be safe in his hands but that people would be delighted with my choice. That was not to be.

On my return I was greatly surprised to find general disappointment. There had been no major disasters, the church hadn't fallen apart and collapsed. Brian had preached but not up to his usual standard. It was hard to explain, other than that people seemed relieved that we were back and that life could begin again.

Some time later I was preaching at another church some distance from Basingstoke, which required that I was away the whole weekend. Janette stayed at home and that meant I was able to get a first-hand report on my return.

Brian had once again been left in charge, but with my wife present I would have a full, blow-by-blow account, including the fine print. First of all I heard about the things that should have happened but didn't. Visitors who had not been recognised and welcomed, births unannounced, members in hospital not prayed for and, worst of all (in Janette's eyes), no mention that their pastor was away preaching elsewhere—no prayer for him or for our missionaries.

Then followed the list of things which shouldn't have happened. For example, Mary, a patient from the local mental hospital whom I used to call our phantom tambourine player, had taken advantage of my absence. As many charismatics will testify, tambourines can be a mixed blessing. If played properly and to the appropriate tune all well and good. However, handled in the same manner as that of Mary then it becomes more like a weapon, indeed a veritable instrument of torture. Mary never got the beat right, it was always slightly off. It was like singing beside someone who is tone deaf—extremely disconcerting and irritating. She always arrived early for the services so I used to stand on guard like a customs official waiting at the ready to confiscate the dreaded contraband. It was easy to tell whether we were to be favoured with her musical accompaniment because she always carried the tambourine in a large plastic shopping bag. Actually I didn't deprive her of the tambourine; a gentle reminder that only those who were officially recognised as musicians were allowed to play was sufficient. However, I encouraged her that if she practised hard back at the hospital she might yet qualify. Poor nurses, will they ever forgive me?

In my absence Mary had taken full advantage. While the cat was away, the mouse played—and with what relish and gusto!

I tried to help Brian but with little or no success. He knew what was needed but how to handle it was another matter. My problem was that I thought that the ability to lead a congregation was a skill that could be learned by almost everyone. How wrong I was!

Not long after this I was studying the book of Ephesians and in particular chapter 4, when I came across verse 7: 'But to each one of us grace was given according to the measure of Christ's gift.' My attention was riveted by the thought that not only did the word 'measure' imply a certain quantity but also a limitation. In other words, if Christ deposited in me the grace to function as a pastor then I was limited, restricted to operate within that ability. So when I wandered into the field of a prophet I was in fact off limits. It would be trespassing!

Suddenly I saw the light. Now I understood why Brian couldn't do it. He didn't have grace for it. I was pushing him into a field of responsibility that was off limits. One wouldn't accept the kind offer of an electrician to pull an aching tooth, nor would one request a plumber's help in clearing a bowel blockage. Why should I ask a Christ-gifted teacher to act like a pastor?

Someone once asked me the question, 'So where does training fit in? God's gifting doesn't preclude the need for it, surely?' The answer is: of course not. If a person has the grace for a particular ministry, then you can disciple them towards a more mature exercising of that ministry, but if they do not already have God's gift of grace for it then you can't. I and many other apostolic leaders have tried and have discovered it doesn't work.

I took some quality time with Brian during which I explained my discovery in Ephesians 4 and carefully affirmed the grace gift of teaching which I could see Christ had deposited in him.

I then asked his forgiveness for assigning to him and requiring from him a service for which God hadn't given him grace. I released him to specialise in studying in order to be the recognised Bible teacher in our church. Today he is one of my favourite Bible teachers; he always feeds me with fresh insights and has the knack of stimulating my faith and confidence in Jesus.

Brian's situation is not an isolated one. It is bad enough that so many clergy are either unregenerate liberals or immoral—sometimes both—but when the rest of the pulpits are occupied by so many born-again, Bible-believing square pegs in round holes it is difficult to see how God will ever be glorified in his twentieth-century church.

Some experts suggest that over 50 per cent of church leaders are functioning outside their gifting. If that is true there must be an awful lot of joyless, frustrated, unfulfilled Christians sitting in half-empty church buildings Sunday by Sunday. Of course, most denominations only make room for the office of pastor and only provide formal training for pastors and teachers. Some seminaries include a little training for evangelism, but that is not the same as training an evangelist, and there is no seminary training for prophets even though the Bible speaks about 'schools' of them.

If a person's gift is that of an evangelist he or she is forced to join a para-church organisation to fulfil his or her calling. But the poor unfortunate prophet has no hope whatsoever, other than to accept the pastorate of a church and exercise his prophetic calling through the office of a pastor—all of which is a recipe for disaster, as was the case of Bill, a prophet in pastor's clothing.

When I first met him the frustration was already beginning to tell. He was a great preacher so consequently he had a large and growing church—in fact it was the largest in that nation, which only compounded the problem. It was a problem of which he was only too well aware. His eyes filled with tears as he related the details of his unrelenting struggle in trying to do what was expected from a pastor but for which he had no grace. I heard recently that the church is but a shadow of its former self.

I am sorry to sound such a negative note at the outset, but it is a solemn fact that when I raise this issue at leader's seminars and conferences, I get more response from this teaching than any other.

Have you ever wondered why there is such a sharp difference between the numbers of renewed ministers and that of renewed churches? One would have thought that if the leader experienced the blessing of the Spirit he could automatically lead the congregation into the same blessing, but this is not the case.

Being filled with the Holy Spirit does not switch you from a prophet to a pastor, nor from an evangelist to a teacher. The blessing of the Spirit anoints you to do what you have been gifted to do. The square peg remains a square peg, anointed with the Spirit or not.

Back in 1972 I was so exercised about this that I organised an annual leaders' conference called 'Our Generation'.

The purpose was to help leaders who were newly Spirit-filled to bring about the necessary change in their churches, thus allowing the church to be renewed, revitalised and restored. In other words, I wanted to help them create a new wineskin in order to safely contain the new wine. The results were rather interesting as well as disappointing. Those men who had the pastoral gifting plus the helmsman gift of 1 Corinthians 12 were able to see their congregations make the change; those who were prophets or teachers failed. The conferences served to help these helmsmen pastors but only increased the frustration of the others.

I am frequently asked if there is any hope of change in the denominations and I have reluctantly come to the conclusion that there isn't. The price is too high, the bureaucracy so complicated, the denomination's own civil service has too great a vested interest. There are too many sacred cows. The annual assemblies or synods mostly major in minors, and when they do tackle something heavy like freemasonry or homosexuality among clergy, they usually stop short for political reasons from dealing with it thoroughly. So, sadly, we continue to observe the increasing decline and decay of religion in our nation while its leaders trifle with side issues. Bob Mumford describes the situation accurately when he likens them to stewards rearranging the deckchairs on the *Titanic* as it slowly sinks to the bottom of the Atlantic.

However, for the man who is serious enough (and you may be) there definitely is hope. But first of all we need to ensure that you really aren't a square peg in a round hole. Let us look at a few symptoms.

3

Square-peg Symptoms

Sitting uncomfortably

A square peg—we'll call him James—is never quite comfortable. He is like David, who started out to fight Goliath wearing Saul's armour, a man wearing an ill-fitting suit of clothes—he doesn't look right in them, nor does he feel right. We have all attended a meeting at some time in our lives where the organist didn't have the ability to produce the goods or the praise leader stumbled from song to song winding us up with such choice exhortations as, 'Let's sing this as if we really mean it' (were we all just pretending before?), or, 'Let's really raise the roof.' It's no different with James as the leader. He looks awkward, he is diffident, he is not sure of himself; therefore he is half-hearted. James frequently comes up with new schemes he's either picked up at leaders' conferences or from the latest Christian bestseller he's been reading, but they lie shallow in his mind and carry no deep heart conviction. Fortunately most of these bright ideas never get further than the elders' or deacons' meetings, and those which do get inflicted upon the unsuspecting and unresponsive congregation usually go off like a damp squib. In a nutshell, he is programme-orientated. You can drop programmes and schemes—they are all expendable—but deep convictions born out of revelation can never be discarded; there is no room for compromise.

James will return from renewal conferences unusually perky but it is only a flash in the pan. After two Sundays he is back to his usual awkward, uncomfortable self, which he covers up of course with a strained smile or a slight whine in the voice to denote sincerity. You seldom ever get good strong eye contact with James; he is too insecure and uncomfortable.

Absence of joy

James struggles to be successful. Not surprisingly he has an identity crisis which drives him to fish for approval. He knows he is gradually losing the people's confidence and suspects, not without reason, that people are talking negatively about him. As job satisfaction is an essential ingredient which makes up a man's sense of total well-being and happiness, it is no wonder that not much joy seems to radiate on James' countenance. What you sow you reap, that's a divine principle. If a leader sows heaviness, uncertainty and hopelessness, that's exactly what he will reap in the people. So James ends up with a joyless congregation—but not all the time. Should they have an evangelistic crusade (and most evangelists are joyful, bouncy, positive, larger-than-life people), the saints come alive, which only adds to James' problem. He may put on a brave smile but deep down his insecurity is increasing, especially when some of the folk ask him, 'Can we have the evangelist back as soon as possible?' adding, 'Why can't we have meetings like this all the time?'

Barrenness

If you present to me a leader like James I can almost guarantee you will find a congregation that is virtually unresponsive. To put it bluntly, he just doesn't light their fire, he is unable to motivate them into action. Take for example the prayer meeting. If James succeeds in getting people there, that's only half the battle. Getting them to take part is another matter and that is where one of James' little schemes comes in handy.

'Tonight we are going to have one-sentence prayers starting with you, Lily, and then right around the circle.' Every church has a Lily. She's worn that same bonnet for years, except for the less formal occasions, in which case it's the thick, woollen, large-needle, knitted one, pulled firmly down round the ears.

One thing you can say for Lily—she's faithful. You can count on her even under the most arctic conditions! We had a Lily at the Brethren assembly in which I was raised. She seemed always to have a dew-drop dangling on the end of her nose. The highlight of my Sunday morning was when the single communion cup came round. I waited with eager anticipation and baited breath to see whether it dropped in the glass. It usually did. Was I glad children were not allowed to participate in the breaking of bread service!

James is like a cork in the bottle. It seems that people are unable to rise and meet the challenge he sets before them. At the same time he feels like he is swimming the breaststroke in a sea of peanut butter, which leads us to the next symptom.

Frustration—leading to irritability

The *Merriam-Webster Dictionary* defines the word 'frustrate': 'To balk in an endeavour' or, 'to bring to nothing.' That's just how James feels and it frustrates him.

Most people in his care may not be aware of it but his wife and children are, especially if they dare suggest ideas that might make an improvement. Eventually the saints begin to recognise all is not well. Instead of giving them encouragement and approbation, he chastens them as part of the message. His teaching has an emphasis that is more man-centred than Christ-centred. Naturally there are times a leader needs to make an application that is particular and relevant to his audience, but I am thinking of the situation where the subject seems to be placed on a treadmill and not removed. He is trapped in a negative interpretation and application of Scripture. John Noble calls it 'sheep bashing'—an apt description.

Just imagine having Thomas and his supply of faith in your diaconate, together with Peter whose little toe is all that peeps out of the corner of his mouth, not to mention James and John ably supported by their mother. Yet Jesus showed not an ounce of frustration; on the contrary he commends them to his Father saying, 'They have kept Thy word.' At the same time he acknowledges they were a gift: 'Thine they were, and Thou gavest them to Me.'

Weariness

Nothing tires a leader more than unresolved problems, unfruitful ministry and general frustration. Some years ago, while participating in a Bible week conference, I met a pastor who was an old friend. I noticed that he appeared rather downcast.

He asked if I could spare him an hour, so we fixed a suitable time. He had also asked if Bryn Jones, one of the speakers, could join us. I had always observed him to be joyous and outgoing but now an unhealthy heaviness had a hold on him. This depression began to develop soon after his elders had laid hands on him, commissioning him to the office of an apostle. He complained of always feeling tired, of dreading having to get up in the morning to face another day, loss of joy, frustration, lack of confidence—the symptoms were self-evident. Bryn was very frank and told him, 'You are trying to do something God hasn't given you grace for, and if it isn't God's supply you are using it must be your own.' It is most important that we never forget God's work can only be accomplished God's way and with God's resources. The Almighty has some pretty strong things to say about those who hew their own cisterns or wells. He describes it as committing an evil and warns that you are wasting your time and energy because the result will be a broken cistern that can hold no water. We assured him the elders had meant well but were motivated out of a desire to see him enlarged. They had not heard from God.

We encouraged him to return to that which he enjoyed doing the most, namely to pastor the flock of God. Tears of relief filled his eyes. Buried floods in subterranean caverns filled with disappointment, failure and frustration now erupted in deep sobs. It was so good to see him a few days later back to his old carefree self—shoulders back, head up with a sparkle in the eyes. He could laugh and chuckle again. Indeed, like the psalmist he could say, 'My soul is escaped like a bird out of the snare.' For that is what our previous example, James, really feels. He feels like a trapped bird.

I wish every leader and aspiring leader would read a little book jointly written by Dr Laurence J. Peter and Raymond Hull, published by Bantam Books, called *The Peter Principle*. In the introduction Hull writes, 'I have noticed that with few exceptions men bungle their affairs. Everywhere I see incompetence rampant, incompetence triumphant.' The root cause, he claims, is that 'In a hierarchy every employee tends to rise to his level of incompetency' and there he remains bungling along. Because he succeeded at all the previous levels he won promotion to the next, but he reached his limit at the previous promotion. The latest has taken him beyond his ability and into incompetency, so now he's a failure. In the business world he gets tired, but in nationalised industry, state-run institutions, civil service, police, armed forces, or voluntary organisations, he stays.

Having served in the Metropolitan Police for just on

ten years, I can remember vividly men who, through passing a written exam, were promoted from being useful constables to incompetent sergeants. There they stayed, bungling along until they completed their twenty-five or thirty years service. They were a total liability on the force. Sad to say, the same syndrome is also rife in the church, especially in those that have developed house fellowships.

A man is seen to be godly, a good follower, faithful, loyal, an excellent husband and father, so he is selected to lead a house fellowship.

It may take as much as two years before it is discovered that he is a disaster, and when that happens he is usually so hurt and discouraged with guilt over his failure that it is almost impossible to lift his head and get him back on track. A good follower does not necessarily make a good leader.

We have almost completed our list of symptoms—we have one to go which is...

Murmuring

People eventually start murmuring (which is the same as gossiping)—they have lost confidence in James and are disillusioned. Those who were not all that committed in the first place start visiting other churches. Others who are in need seek help elsewhere. There also begins to develop a distrust of the senior leaders who appointed him in the first place. So we see a degenerating saga unfold. What started as an error of judgement then proceeded to become an irritant and has now finally progressed into outright sin, for that is the true nature of murmuring. In fact, if sin can be divided into levels of severity, murmuring is division one. Aaron and Miriam discovered that fact when they murmured against their brother Moses (Num 12).

C. Neil Strait says:

Gossip has never been put in the same bag as murder and assassination, but it is in the same family. Gossip assassinates a person's character and when a character is ruined, a bit of possibility and hope are taken away from a man, both of which are death to dreams and ambitions.

We are reminded in the book of Proverbs there are 'six things which the Lord hates, seven which are an abomination to him: . . . a man who sows discord among brothers.' (Prov 6:16,19, RSV). This calls for radical surgery.

The answer is obvious: James must resign. But how he is handled through the process is most important.

Hindrances

Probably the most potentially serious hindrance to solving the problem is James' wife. Her husband is not only her security but also a key part of her identity. She bears his name as well as his children. When he is successful she feels good. Her life may be almost totally bound up in his. Her perspective amounts to this: her loyal, godly husband is being unfairly treated and dishonoured which, of course, means she is dishonoured. He did his very best and in any case he was only doing what the church invited him to do. The fact is that she stands a very good chance of being scandalised. So severe is the trauma she may take years to recover, if she ever does.

All of this is extremely important to take into consideration, especially in the light of one other interesting phenomenon. The people, who at one time murmured against James and were so disgruntled, now that he is no longer their leader switch their loyalties. They become strangely sympathetic and defensive of him.

Adding to their growing distrust is the development of hawk's eyes focused on any mistakes the senior leaders may make. Before, they may have observed James' errors with binoculars, but now, armed instead with microscopes, everything is examined in minute detail. Just wait until the financial statement is presented at the annual general meeting, not to mention how harsh and authoritarian the senior leaders now appear to be! Here is a situation that is potentially explosive. If James' wife and this group of new-found supporters ever get connected, not only can they be rather bothersome but they have the chemistry to cause a major split in the church. Wisdom and tenderness are greatly needed if severe catastrophe is to be avoided.

Resolution

If you identify with James, settle the issue once and for all and don't play games; grit your teeth and resolve you will not turn back. It is most important that you sit down with your wife and discuss the whole matter carefully. You have it in your power to evoke in your wife strong feelings of resentment towards the church or senior leaders which could inflict permanent damage to her both spiritually and psychologically, or you could make this a great opportunity to show her she's married to a real man with broad shoulders. Remember, how you respond determines how she responds!

Don't blame anyone but yourself. You accepted the position offered, and you alone are responsible for your actions. Treat it as a learning experience and add it to your reservoir of distilled wisdom. Your proper response out of your love for God ensures that God will cause this painful episode to work together for good; both for you and others. Now is the time to move forward; regard today as the first day of the rest of your life. Actions speak louder than words so don't crawl into a hole. In the meetings sit as close to the front as possible, come with the intention of participating and stand tall. Don't allow your wife to mother you nor your friends to defend you. When they do they actually dishonour you. And don't allow negative conversation on your behalf. If you keep to this I can promise you positive feelings of well-being. I can say this with confidence because that's what God told Cain when speaking of his face. He said, 'It can be bright with joy if you will do what you should' (Gen 4:7, TLB).

One certain way to ensure there is no turning back is to open your heart to someone. If you hold the position of senior leader, then ask the Holy Spirit to lead you to someone of stature, perhaps someone who has a translocal ministry and who, under God, has built up a work successfully.

If you are a house fellowship leader go to your pastor and share your decision with him. One final word: if you can possibly manage it I would encourage you to break the news to the house fellowship or congregation yourself. It will reduce the chance of misunderstanding to a bare minimum.

The following story is the account of one man, Steven May-Miller, and how he coped with the painful discovery some years ago that he was a square peg in a round hole.

Restoration of 'failed' leadership

'This is a summary of the lessons God has taught me through giving up the leadership of a 100-member church a few years ago. There were good reasons for handing over the leadership to an older, more experienced man who could devote his energies full time instead of my evenings and weekends. The two years I had given to the task had drained my emotional and spiritual energy; I had lost confidence in myself, and there were new tasks awaiting me.

'Whether or not I had "failed" was not the issue. I knew the time was right to embark upon a new phase in my life. However, the feelings of failure grew within me and remained for many months; the pain of feeling that I hadn't given of my best gnawed away at me for a long time. The Enemy has many ways of keeping Christ's troops out of the battle and he used several tricks on me. Here are some of the things I've learned.

1. The process of restoration is in God's hands, but I can do a lot to help

'Ultimately, God is the One who heals and restores. He usually takes time to allow a gradual inner rebuilding; in this sense, there is nothing I can do to change things. On the other hand, there are certain things which God requires of me. My first responsibility is to check my attitude. Am I taking a negative view of my circumstances, allowing myself to become self-centred and losing sight of Jesus the Lord? An act of the will is required, which will allow God to move in the way he wants to.

2. God is sovereign

'I have made some big mistakes, but God has never made even the smallest mistake. In a miraculous way far beyond my understanding, all our mistakes and failures come under the umbrella of his supreme sovereignty and lordship; he has purpose in every phase of my life and he has prepared lessons in all the moments of failure and despair. At the time, encouragement with phrases like "God will use it" and "adding to the depth of your future ministry" seemed very empty—but they were true, and this realisation has only dawned fully as it has been proved in real life two-to-three years later.

3. The Bible is full of 'failures'

'But God didn't count them as failures. David spent years in the company of villains while being persecuted by Saul; at the height of his success he fell into major sin; he was ousted by his own son whom he had to fight in battle; the son who succeeded him did not follow his father's commands. But David had a heart after God, he pleased him, loved him and worshipped him. And Jesus was called the Son of David! It is not what happened to David, it is how

he handled it. "David found strength in the Lord his God"
(1 Sam 30:6, NIV).

4. Beware self-pity

'It was the biggest pitfall for me as I found my way
through to a full and active place again. It is a natural
thing to try to analyse what went wrong, how I could have
avoided mistakes, and so on. The problem is that this can
lead to self-centredness. I can always find an excuse for
self-pity, but people who feel sorry for themselves are bad
company and bad for themselves.

5. Get back into the action

'When I handed over the church to a new leader, I got
busy with the task of supporting him and helping in whatever way I could. This helped to maintain stability among
the people in the church during a transitional time, it
helped to establish the new leader, it maintained my self-
worth, and most important for me, it kept my thoughts
and focus away from me. There is a big lesson to be
learned from the fact that David's sin with Bathsheba
would never have happened if he had gone out to fight
with his army.

6. Walk close with Jesus

'There is no greater lesson for me than this. A close,
intimate, personal relationship with Jesus and genuine
communion with him is vital always—you can't suddenly
find a strong prayer life in a moment of crisis, it must be
there all the time. I wish I had dug some deeper foundations in this area, and now I'm busy putting it right. A
common reaction in a "failure" or crisis situation is to feel
that God isn't there. However, even if he is not talking, he
is certainly listening as you cry out in pain, need or desper-
ation.

7. I need to know my limitations

'For several years, it seemed that I had carried out every task required of me in the church with success and anointing. When this failed to continue, I couldn't understand why. God has shown me my limitations (for that period of my life) and he has begun to teach me that I will only achieve genuine success when I act out of my weakness and full dependence on him. "For when I am weak, then I am strong" (2 Cor 12:10).

8. Personal accountability

' "Failure" times seem to be an opportunity to put the blame somewhere else. I have found it is right and proper to recognise personal mistakes, without sinking into self-centredness and pity.

9. My identity comes from my relationship with Christ

'My salvation, sonship and inheritance is unaffected by rank, success and other signs. That is one reason why my walk with Jesus, mentioned earlier, is so vital. If my self-worth and identity is elsewhere, it will fluctuate along with the circumstances. But it can be stable, because God is unchanging.

My wife's perspective

'Ann walked closely and faithfully with me through all my experiences. By God's grace, she was not sucked into the same despair that I experienced at times. We have both found how vital it is to talk through what is going on, to be open and honest while encouraging each other to stand firm and "fight the good fight of faith" rather than sympathise with each other's problems and pull one another into self-pity. Ann found great comfort in sharing her experiences with a group of leaders' wives—a group to which she belonged both while I was in leadership and afterwards. They were more than a house fellowship, they were peers who understood the pressures and experiences

she was going through. She needed to talk out those
experiences with someone other than me.

What could the leaders do?

'Probably the most important thing that the church
around me did was to continue to involve me and give the
same recognition and respect as before.

I continued to sit in on elders' meetings as I had previously. I continued to play a full part in leaders' meetings
and in leading church meetings. I was not allowed to
withdraw. At that time I needed recognition and approbation, and this was balanced so that it was never overdone.
That could have pushed me towards a more self-centred,
problem-orientated attitude.

The greatest thing in all my life

'There has been no greater lesson for me in this experience than to learn that my relationship with Jesus is
supreme. No other consideration, activity or person
comes close. In him I find strength, faith, life, courage,
worth and identity.'

Now comes the most important phase of your future ministry, which is to accurately discover what God has given
you grace for. You cannot afford to make the same mistake twice.

4

Discovering Your Gift

It is our prime responsibility to pursue God. The fruit of that intimate communion with the Lord will be his love being poured into our hearts as well as his character being formed in our lives.

There is always the danger of seeking the gift instead of pursuing the Giver, but Paul hits the right balance when he exhorts the Corinthian church, 'Pursue love, yet desire earnestly spiritual gifts' (1 Cor 14:1).

It is important, however, as we endeavour to get our priorities straight, that we also try to understand the measure of grace and the measure of faith that God has deposited in our lives. It is a measure of grace and faith that didn't get there because of our godly character, or lack of it. It is there simply because of God's sovereign goodness.

In Romans 12:3 Paul writes:

> For through the grace given to me I say to every man among you not to think more highly of himself than he ought to think; but to think so as to have sound judgment, as God has allotted to each a measure of faith.

And he continues in verse 6: 'And since we have gifts that differ according to the grace given to us, let each exercise them accordingly.'

So bearing in mind that there is the danger of too much self-analysis, as well as the risk of getting boxed into a narrow confined ministry extreme, let us nevertheless look at some of the pointers that might help us to discover our gift or, as some people put it, our God-given strengths.

The negative accentuates the positive

This exercise is a process of elimination. Labour for the Lord that makes one feel anxious, awkward and weary before you even start, or gives neither joy, sense of fulfilment or satisfaction, must beg the question: 'Has God given grace for that activity?' Jesus said, 'My yoke is easy, and My load is light' (Mt 11:30).

Good questions to ask oneself are: 'Am I sitting down in this thing comfortably?' If not: 'Then why am I doing this?'

A need does not constitute a door of opportunity; only the Lord has the right to decide such matters.

How am I viewed by others?

On one occasion I sat in a circle of nineteen leaders. We were taking it in turns to sit in the hot seat while the others told us what they thought our primary gift was. The options were pioneers, settlers and equippers. Of one man eighteen said he was a pioneer, but despite all our arguments to the contrary he insisted he was an equipper.

It is crucially important that we take careful note of how others view us. Their opinions, although not binding, will give us a good idea of our areas of competency.

A leader can always be identified by whether or not there is anyone following him. I have come to have increasing confidence in how the saints view us, especially when it comes to assessing the suitability of a potential leader.

Theologically, I cannot see that the church is to be ruled democratically, but I am convinced that the mind of Christ is revealed through the corporate body, especially when it comes to recognising a person's gifting. The saints know the difference between ministry that is alive and anointed and that which is not.

Fruitfulness

'You will know them by their fruits' (Mt 7:16). Jesus was giving instruction on how to recognise a false prophet. The church of Ephesus in Revelation chapter 2 was commended by the Lord Jesus because they tested the claims of those who asserted they were apostles. A person who claims to be an evangelist but never leads anyone to Christ is obviously deceived. Someone who thinks he is a teacher but sends everyone to sleep, or is so confusing that most people are left wondering 'What on earth was he on about?' is clearly suffering from delusions.

Prophetic indications

Ben Moore, an American preacher and dear friend, was ordained by his father to the Baptist ministry when he was only seventeen. His dad, who was also a Baptist pastor, quite unexpectedly prophesied over Ben from Luke 4:18 declaring that his ministry would be particularly centred on those oppressed by the devil and bound by curses. I know of no one God uses more effectively to set people free from Satan's power than Ben.

My life-flow in serving God is pastoral. Giving encouragement is one of the main planks in the foundation of pastoral ministry. My parents named me Barnabas, which means 'son of encouragement'. The knowledge of their choice has constantly provoked me to be an encourager of others.

God has also called me to be a spiritual father, which is

an awesome responsibility. This has been confirmed prophetically a number of times; none so dramatic or with greater impact than an incident involving John Hutchinson, one-time proprietor of Torbay Court, Paignton, in Devon. One day, while passing through Basingstoke, John dropped in on me with his son Stephen. We were sitting drinking tea together and chatting about things in general when suddenly John announced, 'Barney, God has just given me a word for you. It's Ezra 2:10.

'What does it say?' I asked.

'I don't know,' he replied, but turning to Stephen he said, 'Look it up, son, I don't have my glasses handy.'

Stephen found the chapter and let out a groan. 'What's the matter?' John asked. 'Is it one of those long genealogy lists?'

'I'm afraid it is, Dad,' said Stephen.

'Well, read it anyway,' John asked with an air of resignation, so Stephen found the verse and began to read, 'Now Bani had 642 sons.'

Amid the laughter and mock wiping of the brow, I knew God was calling me up into a new area of challenging and demanding responsibility.

Since that arresting incident I have received two letters from Third World countries addressed to Pastor Bani Coombs!

John the Baptist was prophesied over by his father Zacharias in Luke 1:76 when he said, 'And you, child, will be called the prophet of the Most High; for you will go on before the Lord to prepare His ways.'

Paul exhorts Timothy in 1 Timothy 4:14, 'Do not neglect the spiritual gift within you, which was bestowed upon you through prophetic utterance with the laying on of hands by the presbytery.'

Prophecy is an important method that God uses to help us discover our gift and is not to be despised. Of course it needs to be tested, but never despised.

The Scriptures

Lastly, there are times when God speaks directly to our hearts through our reading of the Scriptures.

It was in such a manner that I came to leave the Metropolitan Police. It was past midnight when it happened, I had got off duty late due to arresting a man for stealing. Janette had already retired to bed, so feeling hungry I went into the kitchen, made myself a cup of coffee and began eating a bowl of cornflakes. I took my Bible and began reading Isaiah 52. Suddenly I came to verses 11 and 12:

> Depart, depart, go out from there, touch nothing unclean; go out of the midst of her, purify yourselves, you who carry the vessels of the Lord. But you will not go out in haste, nor will you go as fugitives; for the Lord will go before you, and the God of Israel will be your rear guard.

Don't ask me how I knew, because I would be unable to explain it; all I can say is, I knew the Lord was telling me, 'I want you to leave the police and give yourself to pastoring my people.' Initially I received much discouragement from well-meaning saints, one of whom thought I would do better if I stayed in the police until I qualified for my pension, then I could be independent and wouldn't be a burden on God's people! But despite this I have given myself to the ministry of pastoring God's flock for the past twenty-six years.

Many, if not most, pastors can point to a similar encounter with the Lord as they were reading the Bible. Faith comes by hearing.

We need to be assured that what we are engaged in is not some good idea of our own making but that God has placed his hand on our lives and put his grace in our hearts and commissioned us into his service.

5

He Who Serves, Leads

The late Arthur Wallis, Bible teacher and author, was an officer in the British army during World War II. Some years ago he related how the officers at Sandhurst were instructed to lead their men by example. For instance, if a challenge was set before the platoon, the officer in charge had to accomplish it first or participate in the exercise alongside them.

A regular activity was the ten-mile route-march with full pack on the back weighing 56lb, plus rifle. By the time they returned to barracks, most of the soldiers were exhausted and near to the point of collapse. The platoon leader's first task was to examine carefully the feet of all the men, often helping to pull their boots off, then to ensure that they all had a mug of tea. Lastly, those whose blisters had burst and had deteriorated into a bloody mess were dispatched to the medical officer for treatment. Finally, when—and only when—all his men were comfortable, he would take off his own boots and enjoy a mug of tea with them.

Jesus gave extremely clear instructions to his apostles regarding how they were to exercise authority. They were not to use it like the kings of the Gentiles who lorded it over their subjects in a condescending, patronising manner. This style portrayed them as benefactors, but the greatest was to conduct himself as if he were the youngest and the leader as if he were the servant. Jesus made it abundantly clear both by words and actions that he came not to be served but to serve.

Take for instance the night Jesus was betrayed. We find him spending his remaining hours having a meal with his disciples, who also happened to include Judas. The custom was for a servant to wash the feet of each one as he entered the house—an extremely menial task—but apparently no servants were present. So the meal commences with each person's feet remaining unwashed. Suddenly, in the middle of the mealtime, Jesus stands up, removes his top garment, takes a towel, wraps it round his waist, pours water into a bowl and one by one washes the disciples' feet. Apart from Calvary, this was servant leadership at its most dramatic and at its greatest expression. The One who put billions of galaxies of stars into space stooped to wash, dirty, sweaty feet!

There is a certain style of leadership that is characterised by dominating, bullying tactics. Stalin, whose use of violence and fear was probably unsurpassed in modern history, kept control of most of Eastern Europe using such methods.

Some will rule and keep control by an intimidating use of words, a menacing tone of voice or a particular facial expression of disapproval. There is also a more acceptable form of leadership that exists, especially among Christians, due to the charisma, vision and confidence the leader exudes. People follow him because he 'scratches where they itch'. They believe he will take them to the promised land.

He can get away with rudeness, arrogance and conceit as well as the flaunting of his affluence because the eyes of his naive followers are blinded by his ability to fire their imaginations. He offers them a way out of their mundane, humdrum, boring existence into what appears to be a spiritual utopia. Yet none of this is acceptable to God.

Consider Mother Teresa, Nobel Peace Prize winner and an outstanding celebrity on this world's stage. She is held in such high esteem that our queen and prime minister would readily rearrange their schedules, put out the red carpet and feel greatly honoured if this humble, diminutive elderly lady asked to see them at short notice. She has no letters after her name, nor has she written any books; it is simply that she loves. Her love for Jesus has caused her to give her life in serving the most despised, unloved and rejected of India's poor. All she does is to offer love and tenderness, to wash and clean filthy open sores, to touch those in her care and speak comforting words, as well as to give them a bed to sleep on. In this way she can lead them to her Saviour and allow them to die with dignity.

The most powerful and respected leaders are those who serve the people in their care. The story is told of a certain dean of a small college in Pennsylvania. On one occasion it was reported to him that the walls of one of the men's dormitories were smeared with shaving cream, peanut butter and jelly. As he proceeded to make investigations he met with surprised innocence from each student. No one claimed to know anything at all about it!

There were several courses of action open to him. He could have insisted that the students each gave a hand to clear the mess; he could have called the caretaker who would certainly have dealt with it, despite the lateness of the hour. However, the dean chose a third and very different course of action. He went and got a bucket and brush and set to work on the walls himself. Word was quickly passed around until one by one every student was aware that their dean was scrubbing the walls. Soon he was no longer working alone as his example spoke to the students. He did not demand respect, but through his servanthood he certainly commanded it.

Jesus said, 'If I then, the Lord and Teacher, washed your feet, you also ought to wash one another's feet' (Jn

13:14). He was described in Isaiah 42:1 as 'My Servant'. What an accurate description! He evidently served his earthly father, Joseph, in the carpenter's shop. Throughout his three and a half years' ministry he healed the sick and cast out demons, thereby constantly ministering to the needs of people. But, some may say, 'He was only setting an example before his disciples; it would be different now.' Would it? Let facts speak for themselves. Here is Jesus after the resurrection. He has conquered both death and the grave. He has disarmed the rulers and authorities of Satan's kingdom and made a public display of them. He could have appeared before his disciples with great pomp and ceremony, accompanied by tens of thousands of angels, cherubim and seraphim all singing of his glory and triumph.

He could have come with lightning, thunder, earthquakes, the splitting of mountains and an almighty display of his shekinah glory filling the sky, but the Lord of glory chose to reveal himself on a beach in lowly Galilee, frying pan in hand, cooking breakfast for his men. Imagine that! The omnipotent, omniscient, eternal King of kings, Lord of heaven and Lord of earth, having all authority in heaven and on earth, bending over a smoky fire, cooking breakfast for his lads!

Later, Jesus ascends to his father's throne to share the glory once again. If he were to spend the rest of eternity basking in the worship and adoration of the redeemed community together with the angels and archangels, it would only have been his proper due. But no, he is still about his Father's business for 'He always lives to make intercession for [us]' (Heb 7:25). Finally, in Luke 12:37 we discover the reward for those whom he finds on the alert when he returns. 'He will gird himself to serve, and have them recline at the table, and will come up and wait on them.' Imagine that—it is beyond our comprehension. The Creator serving the created! The Redeemer waiting on the redeemed! No wonder 'God highly exalted Him, and bestowed on Him the name which is above every name, that at the name of Jesus every knee should bow...and that every tongue should confess that Jesus Christ is Lord' (Phil 2:9–11).

It seems such a difficult lesson to learn, that the way up is down; to gain we must lose; to live we must die; and to lead we must serve. It is patently clear that having a servant's heart is one of the highest qualities a leader can possess.

The people who have made the deepest impression on my life and who have won my respect have been those with a serving disposition. One of my favourites is Campbell McAlpine. Twenty years ago, as a young Baptist pastor, I happened to be staying overnight in his home. That in itself was a great privilege. Early in the morning I awoke to the sound of splashing water. Looking out of the bedroom window I discovered the cause of the noise. It was Campbell, bucket and sponge in hand, attacking the grime on my car, happy as a skylark.

My mother is another who never seems happier than when she is helping others. For years she cooked the meals for two elderly ladies who lived in cottages adjoining her home, even though she was in her seventies herself. The late George McLeod, pastor of the church I attended as a teenager, once made this remark about her, 'I'm not fit to do up her shoe-laces.'

My sister Rebecca and her husband Ron run a home for senior citizens in Herne Bay, Kent. I don't know of anywhere where the elderly are so lovingly and sensitively cared for. Everything revolves around what is most convenient and accommodating for the residents. For instance, usually elderly people get to sleep sometime between 11.30 pm and 1.00 am, yet in most geriatric institutions they are expected to retire to their rooms by 8.00 pm, or even earlier. Not so with Rebecca. At about 10.30 pm they have a nightcap followed by a Bible passage in which they all participate reading. This is concluded by prayer, then off to bed.

Of course it is different for those who wish to retire earlier. For her, it is not a business, it is a ministry of love. Many times she has stayed up all night sitting at the bedside of one of her ladies who was dying, holding her hand until she breathed her last. Most of you reading this book will have never heard of my sister, but God has, and it is all recorded in his book, and what has been done secretly he will one day reward openly.

Last, but not least, God has blessed me with Janette, my wife of thirty-five years. She is not a great public speaker or anything like that, but she has a remarkable, unselfish servant's heart.

Because of the responsibilities I have, people come to our home continuously. Without exaggeration, hundreds of times I have brought people home to have a meal or to stay overnight and each time Janette has uncomplainingly given of her best. One young man I led to Christ was a vagrant so I brought him home to stay with us until he got work and suitable accommodation. Poor Janette, with two young children at the time—she must have despaired at my inconsideration. His clothes were so bad and his body so filthy that it took several days plus a strong disinfectant to eradicate the sickly odour from our bathroom.

In fact, his clothes were so horrible and flea-infested, Janette picked them up with wooden tongs and dropped them straight into the dustbin, and yet not one word of complaint passed her lips.

God has promised that he will give shepherds who are after his own heart, not like those he condemns in Ezekiel 34 who failed to strengthen the sickly, who neglected to heal the diseased, omitted to bind up the broken and abandoned the scattered and lost.

Jesus said, 'The good shepherd lays down His life for the sheep' (Jn 10:11). May God help those of us who are leaders genuinely to serve his flock with great care and in a spirit of humility.

6

Owners or Stewards

We were getting rather anxious to discover new leadership for a number of housegroups. John and Norma were, to all intents and purposes, a totally committed couple and regular attenders at all the meetings. Their three children were well behaved. From any angle you cared to look they appeared ideally suited to be entrusted with responsibility. John's warm, caring temperament and Norma's outgoing vivacious personality seemed perfectly tailored for such responsibility. Since joining the church two years previously nothing had occurred that would have cast any shadow on their suitability.

Our invitation was warmly accepted. Soon they were commissioned with prayer and the laying on of hands. Not the slightest indication existed of the forthcoming trouble.

In arriving at our decision to appoint them leaders we had failed to apply three basic safety precautions. First, we failed to recognise that we were in a hurry. Proverbs 19:2: 'He who makes haste with his feet errs.' A pressing need does not constitute the will of God. More time in prayer might have saved us months of painful unrest.

Second, had we taken the precaution of contacting the pastor of John and Norma's previous church we might have discovered that they had a history of ongoing conflict with church leadership.

Third, during their two years with us, no tension or conflict had existed in the church that might have tested their loyalty; nor had we given them any minor responsibility that could have certified their faithfulness and reliability. One of our building principles is 'Never build too much on someone who is untested.' I am sure this is what Paul was implying in 1 Timothy 3 verses 10 and 13 when he writes, 'And let these also first be tested; then let them serve as deacons if they are beyond reproach,' and 'For those who have served well as deacons obtain for themselves a high standing and great confidence in the faith that is in Christ Jesus.'

At first all the signs were positive, but after a few months troublesome symptoms began to appear which, when put together, added up to the realisation that John and Norma were owners, not stewards.

One thing that is very clear in God's kingdom is that while he loves to delegate stewardship so that we can be 'workers together with God', he never, never releases ownership; it is always retained by him. The earth is the Lord's and all it contains. We can shepherd the sheep but we can never own them. Jesus told Peter, 'Feed my sheep' (Jn 21:16, AV). Paul told the Ephesian elders in Acts 20:28, 'Be on guard for yourselves and for all the flock, among which the Holy Spirit has made you overseers.' Peter, in 1 Peter 5:2, exhorted the elders, 'Shepherd the flock of God among you.' Everything we receive from God remains under his ownership, 'For from Him and through Him and to Him are all things' (Rom 11:36). So we see the gifts are the 'gifts of the Spirit', the fruit is the 'fruit of the Spirit'. The battle is 'the Lord's battle', the armour is 'the armour of God'.

This principle is consistently supported throughout Scripture in phrases such as 'the joy of the Lord', 'the love of God', 'the peace of God', 'the strength of the Lord', 'salvation belongs to our God'.

As leaders we need to guard ourselves against referring

to the congregation as 'my people' or 'my church', or using the expression 'my ministry'. Some may feel all this is inconsequential, but recognising the struggles I have encountered over many years to discipline myself to keep my grubby, fleshly, possessive hands off God's property, I realise I am not the only one who faces this temptation. I have come to feel comfortable with the phrase 'the people God has entrusted to my care', or 'the ministry God has entrusted to me'. We can never be too careful.

Symptoms of ownership

The following are some symptoms usually evident in a person behaving as an owner.

First, he is overprotective of those in his charge, like a mother hen with her chicks. He tends to make excuses for their questionable behaviour, such as absence from meetings, tardiness, lack of participation or enthusiasm. Should the senior leader ask searching questions as to the spiritual status of any particular person in his group he immediately springs to their defence.

Second, he is performance-oriented. When the group has a visiting speaker he usually finds himself all knotted up inside, terrified that something may go wrong. He has already exerted considerable pressure to ensure everyone shows up.

The problem is that his identity is directly linked to the performance of his group, whether it's the choir, youth fellowship, Sunday school class, or congregation.

Third, he is numbers-conscious. Again, it all has to do with his need for recognition. Now God seems to like everything numbered; even one of the books in the Bible is called Numbers! He has included long sections in the Scripture that record the descendants of certain people.

Even the number of hairs on our head is known by God, but God does not need the numbers either for security purposes or for some ego trip. Why is it that we leaders fall into the trap of inflating the figures to impress others? I heard recently of one pastor who, when asked how many he had in his congregation replied, 'Between 3 and 400'. When challenged by another pastor, who happened to know he only had 38, he defended that he had answered honestly: it was between 3 and the number 400!

Fourth, he is possessive. This is hardly surprising seeing that ownership and possessiveness are so similar, but it is worth some consideration. He will be reluctant for someone to go to Bible college or minister elsewhere because he needs everyone to support and strengthen his endeavours. His motives are selfish. He holds on to people through a variety of manipulative controls. Their loyalty can be questioned or even their spirituality. Alternatively, he will plead the burden is too heavy or that it is not the same when they are absent; or he may express plain old disapproval.

An owner handles a group or church like a puppeteer who pulls the strings of a puppet whereas a steward tunes his heart in with what his heavenly Father desires and then leads the people in that direction. An owner pleases himself, a steward seeks to please the one who sends him. Jesus was the perfect example of a steward. He constantly honoured his Father as the source of both his words and his actions. A steward never plagiarises another, he never takes the credit. He is always careful to honour his immediate superior and handle what has been entrusted to him in such a way that it does not draw people to himself in some illegal manner. 'Let a man regard us in this manner, as servants of Christ, and stewards of the mysteries of God. In this case, moreover, it is required of stewards that one be found trustworthy' (1 Cor 4:1–2).

7

The Doughnut-hole Principle

I woke up with a start. Outside it was still dark. I had been dreaming again, but it was not the usual fuzzy type. The dream had been so vivid: a man's hand grasping a gun, his finger ready on the trigger. It was all so clear. Although I had not seen his face I knew whose hand it was. A cold shiver ran up my spine as I pulled the blankets closer about my neck and tried to get back to sleep.

A few days later the phone rang. It was Maurice, the man in my dream.

'Barney, I need to see you urgently; could you come to our house as soon as possible?'

'Sure I can,' I responded and then proceeded to relate to him my dream, ending with, 'and the hand holding the gun was yours'. He gasped audibly, then his voice quivering with emotion, he said, 'If you knew how many times during the past two weeks I have put a gun to my head you would be amazed. I just didn't have the guts to pull the trigger.'

Who was Maurice? An ex-convict? A drug addict? A member of an armed gang? No! He had been a Baptist pastor with a very successful ministry. He was a good preacher with a vibrant personality. On Sunday mornings his church service was packed. Married with two children, he had everything going for him—at least until Liza came on the scene.

She was sixteen years old and had run away from home because she was terrified of her mother—a spiritualist medium. So, with no home and no one to care for her, room was made for her at the Baptist manse. Six months later Maurice abandoned his loving wife and precious children and took off with Liza. It wasn't long before they had a baby. Eighteen months later a second one arrived. Finally, Maurice obtained a divorce and married Liza. At this point they moved to Basingstoke. They came to a few of our services but it was too much for Liza; they stopped coming because she wept uncontrollably throughout each meeting.

Months had passed without seeing them until the telephone call. I immediately drove to their home, mulling over in my mind what I might say when I got there. If God had taken the trouble to warn me in a dream, surely he hadn't given up on Maurice. Coupled with this, I had a deep sense that there was some hidden cause of Maurice's weakness lurking in his past; some major infection that existed long before Liza came into his life. As I drove along I lifted my heart to the Lord for the key that would unlock the situation; gradually a clear impression settled in my mind. Something had happened to Maurice when he was a young teenager that had severely damaged him. I was convinced it was irreparable unless God supernaturally intervened. It had been a time-bomb, slowly ticking away until it exploded.

On my arrival he further explained why he had turned suicidal. Liza had found a new lover; in fact it was a neighbour just a few houses away.

He was even willing, if necessary, to share her but she had made it clear she wanted to leave him now and move in permanently with the other man. I couldn't believe my ears. Maurice had fallen from shepherding God's people to sharing his wife with another man—it was incomprehensible. Even as I write this I cannot help but feel dismay. How could a man throw away the high and holy privilege of serving the Lord of heaven and earth, not to mention forfeiting all the promised blessings of the age to come, just for a few fleeting moments of sexual pleasure? It is beyond my understanding, yet we mortals seem to go on destroying our lives and ministry needlessly.

I related to Maurice my prayer, asking God for the key and the subsequent revelation concerning his youth. This was his response. At thirteen he began to attend a large evangelical Baptist church and soon responded to an appeal to receive Christ as his Saviour. The man who counselled him was the church organist; unfortunately he was also a practising homosexual. After Maurice had finished praying he seduced the lad into committing a sexual act. They continued a homosexual relationship right up to his entrance into Bible college, which meant eight years' indulgence in gross sin.

Satan had successfully ensnared a young man, creating in him a character fault which, left uncorrected, was to rob him constantly of his joy in the Lord as the Accuser relentlessly reminded him of his guilty past. Sadly, Maurice rejected my offer of help and friendship.

Jimmy Swaggart, world-renowned TV evangelist, having been caught with a prostitute, blamed his fall and subsequent public disgrace on a secret addiction to pornography which had constantly dogged his path from his early teens. It was a time-bomb that had been slowly ticking away for over thirty years.

The doughnut-hole principle comes from a sermon I once heard delivered by Bob Mumford, a well-known American Bible teacher. He took the phrase 'you man of God' from 1 Timothy 6:11 and produced this design from the shape of an American doughnut.

Christian leaders tend to relate to one another on the basis of their preaching, church growth, seminars, meetings, ministers' fraternals, prayer or Bible study; all of which we could put into the outer circle under 'of God'.

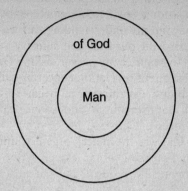

Yet unless we have disciplined ourselves in the area of character there is a hollow centre lacking substance.

We tend either to be impressed or threatened by one another's outward success. Yet how many superstars, not to mention the rest of us ordinary mortals, have hidden time-bombs ticking away waiting for Satan to detonate them?

A friend of mine who pastors a 1,500-member church has a plaque hanging on his study wall which says, 'What success a man builds from his gifting can be destroyed in a moment because of his character.'

Of the fifteen qualifications required for an elder in 1 Timothy chapter 3, only one could be placed in the outer circle of the doughnut; the rest belong to the 'man' part in the centre. Charles Simpson lists them in this manner in his excellent book, *The Challenge to Care*:

1. 'A good report among people outside the church.' King David was judged by God because his sin caused God's name to be blasphemed among the heathen.
2. 'A man with one wife.' This means he must not be a polygamist. This may not seem very relevant in Western

nations but it is a major consideration in African or Middle East countries.

3. 'Temperate' in the exercises of emotions and appetites.

4. 'Prudent'—a leader must possess spiritual wisdom and common sense.

5. 'Admirable'—the leader should epitomise the best qualities of behaviour and evoke esteem both in and out of the church.

6. 'Hospitable'—a leader ought to be gracious and open to receive fellow Christians and strangers alike.

7. 'Able to teach.' In Titus 1:9 Paul expands this qualification. A leader is to hold 'fast the faithful word which is in accordance with the teaching, that he may be able both to exhort in sound doctrine and to refute those who contradict'.

8. 'Not to be addicted to alcohol or other drugs.' Addiction is an appetite out of control and a dependency on something other than the Holy Spirit.

9. 'Gentle'—one who is reasonable and equitable.

10. 'Not a brawler'—argumentative and violent men have no place in the leadership of God's people.

11. 'Not greedy'—greediness is a sure sign of self-centredness.

12. 'One who manages his household well.' One's own house is the first reflection of one's ability to manage.

13. 'One who controls his children with dignity.' There is no place here for a man who controls his children through unrestrained anger.

14. 'Mature and not a novice.' Satan was conceited—impressed with himself. New converts and younger Christians would find it difficult to avoid the trap of conceit if placed in the authoritative role of elder/overseer.

15. 'Humble'—humility is lowliness of mind and freedom from pride.

The Christian world is fairly competent at training people academically and theologically but we are not so good at discipling them in godly character. I have become overwhelmingly convinced that before a man is recognised and released into responsible leadership he needs to have been properly and carefully discipled. This entails the discovering and defusing of time-bombs in a man's character. It also means that character weaknesses are identified and dealt with. Furthermore, every pastor needs a pastor; someone who loves him and prays for him regularly, not only for his ministry but his marriage, his children, his health and his finances. Pastors need prayer especially that God would keep them free from the love of money, from sexual temptation and from fleshly overindulgence. Every pastor needs someone with whom he can share his worries, insecurities, temptations, and yes, when necessary, his sins.

A friend of mine, who is a Christian leader but secularly employed as a manager, was travelling with a lady (also a manager) to their company's three-day residential conference. She also happened to be a fellow-Christian. Halfway along the journey she began to express her attraction for him until finally she placed her hand on his knee.

He stopped the car at the next petrol station explaining that he needed to make a telephone call. As they recommenced their journey she asked him if the telephone call had been urgent. 'Oh yes,' he replied, 'very urgent. I needed to telephone my pastor to tell him there was a lady in my car who was trying to seduce me. I needed him to pray for me.' The atmosphere grew strangely cool and a dangerous situation was averted.

Some people may protest the problem is being overstated. I wish that was the case. Evangelicals retain the notion that moral failures exist to a much greater degree among the liberals. Pentecostals think they are far more prevalent among the charismatics. Sadly, it appears that sin knows no theological or denominational boundaries. *Leadership*, an American magazine for Christian leaders, surveyed its readers regarding moral issues: 61 per cent said they fantasised about having sex with someone other than their wife; 25 per cent said this happened daily or at least weekly; 23 per cent said they had engaged in some form of sexual activity with someone other than their wife since becoming a leader; 12 per cent said it was adultery; 39 per cent thought their fantasising was harmless. Not everyone who falls morally has some deep character fault or time-bomb ticking away waiting to explode. No one is excluded from the magnetic pull of sin. Paul wrote to the Corinthians, 'Let him who thinks he stands take heed lest he fall' (1 Cor 10:12).

I enjoy fishing. Janette and I have built a little cabin on a small island off the west coast of Canada.

There are many dangerous rocks around the island that are exposed only at low tide. I have carefully consulted the marine charts and located them. Needless to say, I take great care in avoiding these areas when out fishing. Likewise there are dangerous rocks scattered about in the sea of life and they lie just beneath the surface; many a good ministry has foundered on their sharp unforgiving points. I would like to show three main areas of danger.

Spiritual affinity

The first one and probably the most deceptive is spiritual affinity. Sertorius Caputa, a Catholic father, made this telling point:

> The devil endeavours first to infuse a love for the virtue of the individual and thus inspire a security that there is no danger. He then excites sentiments of affection for the person and afterwards tempts to sin and thus he causes great havoc.

Saint Thomas said:

> Although carnal affection is dangerous to all it is yet more so for those that associate with persons that seem to be spiritual, for even though the beginning is pure yet frequently famil-

iarity is very dangerous and the more the familiarity increases the more the first motive is weakened and purity is defiled. The devil knows well how to conceal danger. In the beginning he sends out poisoned darts but only those that inflict slight wounds and kindle an affection.

However, in a short time the persons begin to act toward each other not like angels as in the beginning but like beings clothed with flesh. The looks are not immodest but they are frequent and reciprocal, their words appear to be spiritual but are too affectionate. Each begins frequently to desire the company of the other.

Involvement in intercession, the participation of musicians and singers in praise and worship ministry and ministry in deliverance are some of the godly activities where naive believers have fallen prey to the Enemy.

Counselling

The second dangerous area is that of counselling. Repeated counselling sessions with wives of troublesome, unbelieving husbands or single women (especially those recently divorced or widowed) provide unbelievable opportunities for the devil to trap an unsuspecting leader. I shall for ever be indebted to Sid Cheal, a real father in the faith during my mid-twenties, for the sound words of advice he dropped in my ear as we travelled together in the villages of north Hampshire evangelising through the use of literature. He advised, 'Never give lifts to women when you are alone unless it is absolutely necessary old fellow,' and on another occasion, 'Listen, old chap, never counsel women alone. If it's unavoidable always leave the door ajar.'

In twenty-seven years of pastoral ministry I have kept unswervingly to that advice.

Familiarity

Familiarity with lady members of staff is a very dangerous pastime. St Bernard once wrote, 'To be familiar with a woman and to preserve chastity requires greater virtue then to raise a dead man to life.'

The sharing of marriage difficulties and other family concerns; lunch with your secretary or suggestive or flippant remarks provide a conducive atmosphere for the devil to strike a lethal blow.

Lyndon K. McDowell, writing in the USA magazine *Ministry* on the dynamics of ministerial morality, said, 'When any two people of opposite sex work closely together sexual feelings will almost inevitably be aroused.'

I highly commend for your careful consideration the following seven golden rules:

1. Never exchange intimate details with a person of the opposite sex other than your wife.
2. Never put your arm round a woman other than your wife or daughter. Psychologically you are offering them security which just happens to answer one of the deepest needs a woman has.
3. Never counsel a woman alone. If that is not possible, keep the door of the room slightly open.
4. Never give lifts to a woman unless she is old enough to be your mother or it is a matter of urgency. If possible give your wife a telephone call to let her know what is happening; it all helps to keep things in the light.
5. Always ensure your own marriage is in a healthy state—which includes enjoying each other in bed. Proverbs 5:18–19: 'Let your fountain be blessed, and rejoice in the wife of your youth. As a loving hind and graceful doe, let her breasts satisfy you at all times; be exhilarated [literally, intoxicated] always with her love.'
6. Always deal ruthlessly with any deep character fault and without fail confess your problem to a trusted friend; ask him to hold you to strict account for your daily actions

and temptations. One Christian leader arrested by the police for exposing himself in a public place reported by phone every evening for twelve months until his thought patterns surrounding this sexual obsession were broken— strong medicine but big cure!

7. Whenever you find yourself repeatedly thinking about another woman and enjoying the thought, always seek help from a trusted friend, preferably someone you recognise as having spiritual authority in your life.

This applies whether the thoughts are holy or not. It may be that you find yourself longing for her company for whatever deceitful reason your heart may conjure up; or you may find yourself exchanging glances with her. Recognise you are near dangerous rocks that will wreck your life, marriage, family and ministry—unless you take evasive action. Charles Swindoll, pastor of the First Evangelical Free Church of Fullerton, California, has these seven golden rules:

1. Keep the romance in your marriage.
2. Don't take your secretary to lunch.
3. Don't see the opposite sex alone at night.
4. Don't meet them in their homes.
5. Don't sit on their beds in hospital.
6. Don't hold their hands when you talk.
7. Don't put your arms around their shoulders.

Enough said.

8

Take Care How You Build

When I first started as a pastor over twenty-six years ago, it was virtually a one-man show. I announced the hymns, prayed the prayers—except at the midweek prayer meeting—opened and closed the building, did all the preaching and teaching, all the weddings, funerals, infant dedications, hospital visitation and baptisms.

Now baptisms took a little careful planning. I would preach the message, then announce the hymn—it had to be a long one because after singing the first line I would walk to the sidedoor nonchalantly as if I had all the time in the world, then, once out of sight, leap into action like a lunatic and dash to the vestry, tear off my shoes and jacket, pull on a huge pair of waders and don a black baptismal gown. Calmly, I would walk back into the hall dressed like a monk about to go fishing!

I do not know why we bothered because the wretched waders always leaked!

We then proceeded with the baptisms. These were followed by another hymn during which I again walked with the greatest decorum to the sidedoor, then a mad dash to the vestry where my valet the church secretary would desperately attempt to manoeuvre the waders off my feet. It was always an herculean effort with much puffing and blowing—the soaking wet socks didn't help much. Then on with the shoes and jacket and back to the congregation in time to announce the last hymn and give the appeal for people to come forward, either to give their lives to Christ or signify their desire to be obedient to the Lord by being baptised at the next opportunity.

If leaders would stop being 'Jack of all trades' and 'one-man' ministries, the shape and life of the church would change dramatically. The ministry gifts of Ephesians 4:11 are given by Christ so that those with the gifts would equip the saints for the work of the ministry. In that way the body of Christ would be built up.

God's people have got to stop thinking that the church is meetings. We don't go to church, we are the church. Meetings take up at the very most ten hours a week. The church is neither the place we meet nor what we do when we meet. The church is made up of people who have given their lives to Christ in a certain locality and are living out their lives for Jesus twenty-four hours a day, seven days a week. It is a group of these same people joined and committed to one another during sickness and health, poverty or wealth, sadness and joy, the good times and the bad times.

The church of Jesus Christ is a body. Not just like one; it really is one. A body is the physical expression of the person living inside. So it is with Christ and the church. Just as a physical body has many parts, so it is with Christ. The tragedy is that too many church bodies are virtually paralysed, simply because the pastor is shouldering most of the responsibility. It is often the case that the pastor also suffers from the need to be needed.

The pastor has got to stop doing so much of what he presently does and instead delegate it out to the people, who in turn need to take their place. For the whole thing not to end up in a glorified shambles, each person needs to know what his or her gift is in order to function properly, 'According to the proper working of each individual part, [which] causes the growth of the body for the building up of itself in love' (Eph 4:16). You cannot work properly if you don't know what part you are or what gift you have.

A thing or a body?

The church, the body of Christ, is essentially relational. It is a many-membered body. Many leaders from the new churches have great difficulty with the term 'the mystical body of Christ'. Some would regard it as man's invention to cover up the hypocrisy and lack of integrity that exists among so many of us who claim to be Christians. On one occasion in New Zealand I asked a group of ministers what they understood by the term 'the mystical body of Christ'. Not one person was able to give the slightest suggestion of an answer.

The body of Christ is comprised of redeemed people who still retain varying degrees of Adam's fallen nature in their character and personality; so they experience pain as well as joy, loss alongside gain, disappointment as well as fulfilment. The fact is, life in the body is a mixture of pleasure, pain, discouragement, prosperity, poverty, fun, sadness, commitment and broken promises. The body is a group of people who have seen the truth and have a revelation of being committed to one another, knitted together, being built together and held together as members one of another. They are properly functioning parts joined in covenant love to other properly functioning parts. Together they are spiritual joints through which the body is increased.

Once a community of God's people have seen and received this revelation, they do not need to be cajoled, manipulated or coerced into attending any particular meeting. They see that being a part of the body means moving as one.

As children, if we couldn't remember someone's name we called that person 'Thingy'. I cannot think what you would call something that is congregational but unrelational other than a 'thing'. I am reminded of a 'thing' when visiting a fairground with my granddaughter Devon. She loves to ride on the trains. She clambers up excitedly into the front seat and starts turning the steering wheel with great passion. She honks the horn, rings the bell, but it makes not the slightest difference. That old train carries on along the same old track the way it always has. This coming Sunday morning, many pastors and ministers will board their little Baptist, Pentecostal, Anglican or house church train. Just like Devon with her fairground train they will go through all the right motions but that religions 'thing' will carry on in the same old way it always has.

I heard of an amazing incident in a Welsh chapel a few years back. A team of young people from a well-known youth organisation were taking part in the evening service. They all crowded into the minister's vestry to pray prior to the start of the service. Apparently the pastor and deacons all exited into the sanctuary through a particular door on Sunday evenings.

Because the service was being conducted in a different position from normal, the pastor requested that they leave the vestry by a different door. The atmosphere in the room changed dramatically as all eyes shifted on to Mr Jones. He had been a deacon for forty years and had a reputation for disliking change. He was clearly upset with these new arrangements. 'But pastor,' he complained, 'we never go out of that door on a Sunday night.'

'I know,' the pastor replied, 'but with so many young people here I think it would make it easier if we left through the other door.'

Mr Jones was not so easily defeated. 'But pastor, I've been a deacon here for forty years; my father was a deacon here before me, and I can assure you, we have never gone out of that door on a Sunday night.'

'Well,' the pastor sighed, 'I know all that, but I think it's best if we go out of the other door on this occasion. You won't mind will you?'

'Well, I suppose not,' he reluctantly conceded and added in a serious tone, 'but it's highly irregular.' He sat throughout the service, the picture of total misery, arms folded, tight-lipped, eyes blazing. His sacred cow of tradition had been slain.

To a greater or lesser extent there are many Mr Joneses in our congregations.

Congregations that are subtly controlled by people like Mr Jones have no correlation to the type of church Paul wrote of in Ephesians 1:22–23: 'The church, which is His body, the fulness of Him who fills all in all.'

As leaders we need to be far more careful how we build. We need to ensure we are not downgrading the church into a gathering together of a pile of bricks. The living stones God has entrusted to our leadership and care must in reality be 'built together into a dwelling of God in the Spirit' (Eph 2:22).

I am often asked the question: 'How can I know which is the church family to which God wants me to be joined?' My answer always starts like this: 'Find out who and you will know where!' Of course, some people will immediately challenge my reply with, 'But doesn't the Bible tell us not to follow a man?' Well, it does tell us in 1 Corinthians 1:10–12 that it is wrong to have divisions in the local church where people compete with each other saying, 'I am of Paul' and 'I of Apollos' and 'I of Cephas' and 'I of Christ', but in this instance Paul is referring to a divisive party spirit. In contrast to this, three chapters later, Paul exhorts them 'Be imitators of me.'

In the Bible, churches were either identified geographically, as in 1 Thessalonians 1:1, 'To the church of the Thessalonians' (even in these cases clearly Paul is addressing people), or relationally, as in Romans 16:15, 'Greet Philologus and Julia, Nereus and his sister, and Olympas, and all the saints who are with them.'

The next question that frequently follows the first is: 'But how do you know who?' My answer is: 'Who is it who ministers life to you? Who scratches where you itch? Who, when talking with you, gives you the feeling of having a kindred spirit? If this is the Lord joining you together, you will have an immediate sense of feeling at home, both with the leader, and those with him.'

A couple walked into our Sunday morning meeting, and, as it happened, it was their first time with us. They had been searching for a church home for some time but without success. After a time of enjoying the praise and worship and listening to me preach, they turned to each other and simply said, 'This is home.' It was as uncomplicated as that.

A relational body

Building a group of people into a relational body is not easy. It certainly cannot be done by preaching a couple of sermons from Ezekiel's vision of the valley of dry bones.

It is much easier to start from scratch with a new group of people than to restructure an existing congregation. Either way, the leaders need to settle the issue that it will take hard work, together with a great deal of patience and prayer. Apostolic and prophetic input from trusted friends would also make the task more smooth and straightforward.

The example of the leaders is the first and most important key. If they are not walking in love one for another, how can the ordinary rank and file be expected to do it? Besides, the Lord's blessing would certainly be withheld.

The leaders and their families need to meet together socially on a regular basis. I know of some churches where the leaders have never been in each other's homes. They should also regularly meet together for worship and prayer. These times will have a special quality if they are open and vulnerable with each other. The choicest fellowship is experienced when all involved walk in the light. It keeps the heart tender and sensitive both to the Lord as well as each other.

Regular Bible teaching on the subject, delivered clearly and accompanied by up-to-date testimonies, will stir the mind and keep the saints having to face the challenge of either submitting to the Scriptures or hanging on to religious tradition.

Most evangelical charismatic churches are divided into small groups, which greatly helps the church to be relational so long as the prime basis of inclusion is relationship not geography.

These groups give a wonderful opportunity for everyone to be cared for properly, as well as the chance for each person to exercise spiritual gifts. It is the ideal environment for loyalty and trust to develop between close friends, as each person learns how to lay their life down one for another. A balance always needs to be kept between a group growing closer together yet simultaneously having their hearts turned outwards to evangelise and help those who are without Christ.

God is preparing a people that he can dwell in and walk among. Part of our mandate as leaders is to be workers together with him in that great task. One day the fire will reveal whether we have built with wood, hay and stubble or gold, silver and precious stones.

Our great ambition of the ministry entrusted to us ought to be, 'To Him be the glory in the church and in Christ Jesus to all generations forever and ever. Amen' (Eph 3:21).

9

Not Many Fathers

One of the greatest blessings in life a man can have is a spiritual father. Timothy must have experienced indescribable comfort when he received Paul's second letter and read, 'To Timothy, my beloved son...I constantly remember you in my prayers night and day, longing to see you, even as I recall your tears, so that I may be filled with joy' (2 Tim 1:2–4).

Some while ago I sat in a restaurant having lunch with a Baptist pastor and his assistant. With great feeling he told me how some twelve months previously he had begun to enjoy real fathering care from an older minister who lived some 300 miles away. I was quite taken aback when he broke down and cried with uncontrollable sobbing. Pulling himself together he apologised for this emotional outburst explaining that this man had quite suddenly died. He paused, then with his voice beginning to break again, he managed to continue, 'I have longed for this all my life. Just when my hopes were finally being realised it is snatched from my grasp.' He added, 'I feel so bitter.' Although the meal was extremely appetising I could only pick at it, my thoughts retracing what untold blessing had pursued me from a child throughout my entire life.

The first thing to say is that my father truly loved the Lord. His last words to me just five days before he died were, 'Barney, the Lord Jesus gets more precious every day.' He was eighty-six. From the day he became a Christian he was dedicated to serving the Lord.

On Tuesday and Thursday evenings as well as Saturday afternoon and evening, together with my brother-in-law, he would visit the towns and villages surrounding the city of Canterbury in Kent, giving out tracts and sharing the good news with whoever would listen. Often on Saturdays he would take me with him.

Sunday evenings found him preaching in various chapels and mission halls throughout north-east Kent. It was here I began to get used to speaking from the pulpit. He encouraged me to read to the congregation a portion of Scripture and then announce the next hymn. Not satisfied with just that limited exposure he made a small placard, displaying a well-known Bible text, which I was to carry when I accompanied him on his Saturday expeditions. Although greatly embarrassed, those memories have become a treasure chest for me. It was on these trips he would share with me some of his deepest thoughts and closely guarded secrets: his experiences in World War I, his family background and his driving passion to share the gospel with the unchurched. He once said to me, 'You will never find me sitting listening to the gospel being preached when I can get out and preach it myself.' He was still doing so the week he died.

Autograph books were greatly in vogue when I was a youngster. He wrote in mine what he wrote in them all, 'One little life will soon be past. Only what's done for Christ will last.' The apostle Paul said that we have many teachers but not many fathers (1 Cor 4:15). How true!

Sid Cheale, another father in the faith to me, was an evangelist with the European Christian Mission and always active in the Lord's work. Every month he would tour the villages south of the Hampshire town of Basingstoke, distributing *Challenge*, an evangelistic newspaper. As often as I could I would travel down from

London to help. Sid insisted that the paper was delivered personally rather than posted through the letter-box. This was in order that any opportunity to have a chat about the Lord was eagerly seized upon. We used to travel from village to village in his old Land-rover.

I learned so many wise things from the conversations enjoyed as we journeyed from place to place. I now teach others principles and safeguards taught me by this choice man of God. Interestingly enough, at the time I was not aware of how valuable his counsel was. I just enjoyed being with him. Here was a man, out of a father's heart, giving me his time and the benefit of many years of invaluable experience. I am sure he does not realise what he built into me during those casual conversations.

It was in Sid's home that I first talked with W.F.P. Burton, Congo pioneer missionary, who planted nearly 1,500 churches during the 50 years he spent labouring in the gospel. I had previously heard him speak during a communion service at a leaders' retreat. It seems like I can still feel the hot tears running down my cheeks as he spoke of what it cost the Father to give his most precious treasure to bear our sin.

I do not think I have ever felt such love for Jesus as on that memorable morning when I took the bread and wine in my hands. Worship flowed like a river that had burst through a dam. The presence of God was so real you could almost touch him.

Mr Burton visited the church at Basingstoke thereafter on a number of occasions, each time staying in our home. What a treat and what an honour! Having finally finished his ministry in Zaire, he seemed to concentrate his ministry and care on several younger men in the British Isles as well as South Africa. I was privileged to be among them.

He never hesitated to correct me. He could not abide clerical collars and foolishly I wore one, having been requested to do so for a wedding I was to participate in. I was trying to explain where the salad lunch my wife had prepared for him could be found. 'It's no good,' he said, 'I cannot hear a word you are saying with that wretched thing around your throat, go on, go away!' I slunk out of his room like a dog with its tail between its legs, so Janette had to go and explain it all to him.

One of the things he taught that changed the way I prayed was that most prayers in the New Testament are addressed to the Father, plus the fact that Jesus taught when you pray say, 'Our Father.' Another thing Mr Burton taught is, 'When in a disagreement, the least said the soonest forgotten.'

That little bit of advice through over twenty-six years of ministry has saved me from overreacting and stood me in good stead in what could have been many awkward church business meetings or, as we now call them, family forums. It takes two to have a fight, so I find it best never to retaliate. If tempers have flared in a business meeting, God's grace has always been enough to absorb any unkind attack, and if the criticism was true, what had I to lose?

On another occasion I asked Mr Burton's advice, expecting to be severely reprimanded. I had given my first prophetic utterance at one of our meetings, but halfway through had run out of faith and ended up praying. So I shared my problem with him. With a warm twinkle in his eyes he responded, 'I do not see much wrong with that. You could prophesy a little and then pray a bit then go back to prophesying again.' It was just the encouragement I needed.

In my study I have a picture of this great old saint with the words, 'Esteemed very highly in love for his works' sake.' Hanging on our walls are two water-colours painted by him of Congo scenes, but my most treasured possession is the last letter he wrote me just before he died. He liked the Windsor knot that I used when tying my ties but his fingers were no longer nimble. As a result he was unable to do it for himself, so I bought him a couple of ties, put them into Windsor knots so he could just slip the loop over his head and pull it tight round his collar. He was delighted.

His letter thanked me for this kindness shown him and he signed the letter as usual 'W.F.P. Burton', but then rather quaintly he added, 'more frequently Uncle Willie.' He wasn't an uncle; no, he was God's gift to me of a father in the faith.

I was seeking to lead the church at Basingstoke into the life of the Spirit. Many changes were taking place, much to the discomfort of some of the older believers. Mr Burton's presence and the authority with which he spoke, plus the fact that he was older than most of our senior citizens, totally endorsed the steps I was taking, not to mention his public approval of the ministry God had entrusted to me. Spiritual father, pastor or confidant, call him what you will, every pastor needs one.

I met Arthur Wallis for the first time at the same conference as that at which Mr Burton spoke. Over the next few years our lives consistently seemed to cross. I had read his classic on revival, *In the Day of Thy Power*. The more I got to know Arthur the more I appreciated his integrity and spirituality. His counsel, encouragement, as well as correction further added God's discipline into my life. An interesting observation is how many other young pastors found fathering care extended to them from these men already mentioned.

I am convinced that you cannot go like a wine taster to try to select the most godly, wise, discreet, attractive, well-known elderly sage to be your spiritual father; he is a gift from God.

I am equally convinced that if a man genuinely desires God's fathering heart to be expressed to him through mortal flesh and if he is willing to receive whoever God sends him, then what he asks for will be granted according to his measure of faith.

The tragedy is that most young pastors realise too late

how much they need a father-figure in their lives; someone who can trim them back a little. Jesus called it pruning; painful yes, but absolutely necessary. A father-figure is someone who can steer you into depth of ministry rather than breadth. A succulent portion of meat personally discovered is ten times more tasty than one copied from a ministry tape or sermon notes to aid the busy pastor.

Personally I think there is a difference between being a father in the faith and a pastor. Being a father includes pastoral care but yet it is something more—something to do with foundations. Paul said, 'I became your father through the gospel'; 'As a wise master builder I laid a foundation' (1 Cor 3:10). I also consider there to be a difference between the fatherhood of churches and that of a person. Brother Andrew in his book *God's Smuggler* refers to a certain Uncle Hoppy from Dartford in Kent who helped shape his life. I knew this great saint of God. Andrew was not the only individual who received fatherly oversight from him. However, the point I want to make is this: on a personal level he was superb, but not so at a community level. The small group he pastored never really prospered under his leadership.

By contrast the apostle Paul was a father to all the churches he planted. To the Galatians (4:19) he said, 'My children', to the Thessalonians he wrote, 'We were exhorting and encouraging and imploring each one of you as a father would his own children' (1 Thess 2:11). This was corporate fatherhood. In addition he was a personal father in the faith to Timothy and Titus as well as Onesimus. On the other hand, although Paul was a blessing to Epaphroditus he did not regard himself as his spiritual father for he is careful to call him 'My brother and fellow worker and fellow soldier' (Phil 2:25).

What does a father do? Well to start with he is a model, someone you can imitate. Paul was not embarrassed to tell the Corinthians, 'I exhort you...be imitators of me' (1 Cor 4:16). To the Philippians he writes, 'Brethren, join in following my example' (Phil 3:17). To the Thessalonians he says, 'But in order to offer ourselves as a model for you, that you might follow our example' (2 Thess 3:9).

A father warns, urges, charges, encourages, exhorts, instructs, advises, postures, reminds, but he especially gives approbation—puts his hand on your shoulder, whispers in your ear, 'Keep up the good work.' 'Hang in there.' 'Don't take any notice of them. I've known them for years. They treated Michael the same way. You'll never satisfy them.'

I recall during my first year as a pastor one young man was clapping to the beat of a hymn during an evening service. A year later it would have been appropriate, but these were early days and this particular night it sounded hollow as well as being a distraction. I gave a slight indication with my finger, plus a little nod and he got the message that I didn't approve of his efforts. At the door afterwards he was most perturbed, pointing out that I had quenched the Spirit.

He could have made any number of disapproving remarks but this accusation touched my Achilles heel, throwing me into doubt and not a little fear. The last thing I wanted to do was grieve the Holy Spirit, so I returned to the vestry crestfallen and feeling somewhat insecure. Sid Cheale was waiting there, so needing to share with someone whose answer could be trusted, I dumped my feelings and fears on him. Gripping my shoulder he said, 'Listen old fellow, you don't clap hands when you are fishing, that would only frighten the fish away. After you have caught the fish, then you can clap your hands for joy.' It was just the tonic I needed.

Thank God for spiritual fathers!

10

Grace Is Free but Not Cheap

When God wants to drill a man and thrill a man and skill a
    man,
When God wants to mould a man to play the noblest part.
When he yearns with all his heart to build so great and bold a
    man
That all the world shall be amazed, then watch his methods,
    watch his ways
How he ruthlessly perfects whom he royally elects,
How he hammers him and hurts him and with mighty blows
    converts him
Into shapes and forms of clay which only God can understand
While man's tortured heart is crying and he lifts beseeching
    hands.
Yet God bends but never breaks when man's good he under-
    takes.
How he uses whom he chooses and with mighty power infuses
    him
With every act induces him to try his splendour out.
God knows what he's about.

Joni Eareckson Tada
A Step Further (HarperCollins)

Janette and I were attending a Vineyard conference in the
city of Edinburgh in Scotland. During one of the evening
meetings Paul Cain supernaturally called out my name
and gave me an amazing prophetic word. It is difficult to

recall exactly my feelings at the time but, apart from the content of the prophecy, two things clearly remain. First, the incredible kindness of God who, knowing all of my weaknesses, insecurities and inconsistencies, still had a plan for my life which included having a part in the outpouring of his Holy Spirit in the United Kingdom.

The second thing that deeply impacted me and has caused me to feel a special love and appreciation for Paul was the realisation that this prophetic ministry did not come cheaply, but that behind this five-minute word from God were years of costly self-denial and disciplined seeking of God's face.

False expectations

As I travel in various parts of this globe I regularly come across leaders who are discouraged and disillusioned by the price they are having to pay to carry out their ministry. Some of the unexpected troubles they cite include poor living conditions, lack of transport, insensitive senior leaders, insufficient finances, broken promises, unjustified criticism, ingratitude, sickness, weariness, unrelenting disapproval, false accusations and rejection from those in their pastoral care.

It seems they make two fundamental mistakes: one is that they fail to take into account that we are at war with a very real enemy who knows nothing of the Geneva convention; one who is not only ruthless but a very dirty fighter. He will use every means at his disposal, including your best friend. He specialises in wearing us out with unresolved problems. He is still the accuser of the brethren. His main activity revolves around robbing us of our joy in the Lord and causing us to stumble and sin, thus depleting our spiritual, emotional and physical strength.

The second mistake is false expectations; the unrealistic notion that we will experience a trouble-free life because we are serving Jesus. Man's eternal optimism is a strange phenomenon. It possesses an almost divine quality.

It also appears to be omnipresent, at least it can be found in most leaders, not to mention the omnipotent manner in which it overrides the clearest biblical teaching to the contrary. For instance, consider the following statements from Jesus: 'In the world you have tribulation' (Jn 16:33). 'Love your enemies, and pray for those who persecute you' (Mt 5:44). 'Blessed are you when men cast insults at you, and persecute you, and say all kinds of evil against you falsely, on account of Me' (Mt 5:11). 'And you will be hated by all on account of My name' (Mt 10:22). 'Every branch that bears fruit, He prunes it, that it may bear more fruit' (Jn 15:2). That seems like a rather unpleasant procedure.

There is an inviolable principle found in 2 Corinthians 4:12: 'So death works in us, but life in you.' I have written into the margin alongside this verse these words: 'At the point of my death life is released to others'—in other words, it is others' good at my expense. It seems to me, far from promising a problem-free cosy life the Scriptures strongly suggest an uphill, death-to-self struggle. Words like 'wrestle', 'fight', 'endure', 'patience' all describe the journey. The immortal words of Winston Churchill when he addressed the nation on becoming prime minister could easily be spoken to every Christian leader: 'All I can offer you is blood, toil, tears and sweat.' His beloved Clementine expressed it in an even better way when she replied to a rather depressing letter from Winston at the battlefront during World War I. Quoting a poem of Christina Rossetti she wrote:

> Does the road wind up the hill all the way?
> Yes to the very end!
> Will the day's journey take the whole long day?
> From morn to night my friend.

The church down through the centuries has always

suffered persecution. Fox's *Book of Martyrs* bears testimony to this fact. Its record concludes in the nineteenth century but it has been said that, so far, in the twentieth century more people have died for the cause of Christ than in all the previous nineteen centuries put together. We could well take to heart the exhortation that Peter gave to the still infant church of AD 64: 'Dear friends, don't be bewildered or surprised when you go through the fiery trials ahead, for this is no strange, unusual thing that is going to happen to you. Instead, be really glad— because these trials will make you partners with Christ in his suffering' (1 Pet 4:12, TLB). If we are going to escape the painful discovery that nothing comes cheap, we had better take the trouble to read the fine print.

Beware—God's promises can be very costly

A classic example is God's promise to Abram in Genesis 15:18: 'On that day the Lord made a covenant with Abram, saying, "To your descendants I have given this land, from the river of Egypt as far as the great river, the river Euphrates." ' Abram must have been very excited to receive direct from his God such a thrilling prophecy.

What he was totally unaware of was the manner and circumstances by which he would obtain the first piece. In Genesis chapter 23 we read that Sarah died and Abraham needed a place to bury her. For 400 shekels of silver he purchased Ephron's field that was in Machpelah facing Mamre, which later came to be known as Hebron. In reality it cost not only 400 shekels but something of far more value—the life of his sweetheart.

But what about Joseph? He was only a young man of seventeen when he received quite innocently two dreams from God that clearly revealed his parents and his brothers bowing down to him. Naively he informed his brothers of the dreams. Of course, they received this wonderful news with great warmth and immediately wanted to kill him.

His dreams must have seemed like some hollow joke as the horrendous nightmare of being sold into slavery unfolded before him. We cannot imagine the inner turmoil he experienced as he was dragged off in one direction and watched helplessly as his brothers went in the opposite.

In Egypt, as a slave of Potiphar, he was accused by the lady of the house of attempted rape, which resulted in Potiphar committing him to prison.

Some thirteen long years he languished in prison. It must have seemed like an eternity. Psalm 105:18 says, 'They afflicted his feet with fetters, he himself was laid in irons.' Surely he must have thought at times, 'If only I had not had those dreams, they've spelled nothing but trouble.'

God was in it all

Now Joseph was almost certainly unaware that it was God who sent him to Egypt. Psalm 105:17 tells us, 'He sent a man before them, Joseph, who was sold as a slave.' God's plan was slowly unfolding. I once heard it said, 'God doesn't have problems, just timetables.' Two more years of prison passed before Joseph's time came. Through interpreting Pharaoh's dreams he is promoted from prison to prime minister—in just one day! Psalm 105:19 tells us, 'Until the time that his word came to pass, the word of the Lord tested [or refined] him.' Someone once said, 'Beware of receiving a word from God, it's bound to be followed by a large brick aimed in your direction.'

The fact of the matter is Joseph had no small part in our redemption. In Genesis 45:7 he tells his brothers, 'God sent me before you to preserve for you a remnant in the earth, and to keep you alive by a great deliverance.' Judah was one of the brothers whose life was preserved—thus the messianic line was saved and Jesus the Lion of the tribe of Judah sits today in the midst of the throne as a Lamb, newly slain, having purchased our redemption with his blood. Hallelujah for Jesus and hallelujah for Joseph! Death worked in him so that life in the Person of Jesus could come to us.

I am writing this chapter in Zimbabwe having just come from Uganda. At this moment we have twenty people plus twelve children from the churches I relate to who are serving the Lord Jesus in Uganda. The last nine months have not been easy.

These people have experienced three armed robberies (one of which included a gun fight between the robbers and the police), three house breakings, two instances of stealing from cars, one attempted stealing of a car and one person has contracted tuberculosis; not to mention mosquitoes, rats and the occasional deadly cobra. It is not the first time I have had to wipe away tears as I have watched their selfless dedication as day and night they tend to the needs of the chronic sick, extend loving care to the orphans or teach the children in our two schools. Daily they present their bodies as a living sacrifice so that the love of Jesus might be released to people who are desperately trying to recover from sixteen years' unbelievable suffering under the successive regimes of Amin and Obote.

I salute all of you who have forsaken your comfort zones in obedience to the call of our Lord Jesus, who disturbed your comfort so that you might comfort the disturbed.

The scum of the world, the dregs of all things

From time to time I find myself saying, 'How come I never saw that in the Bible before?' Such is the case with regard to the apostle Paul. I am astounded that he endured such persecution, suffering and rejection. He was beaten up on so many occasions he could not remember how many. Five times he was administered the thirty-nine lashes with the cat-o-nine-tails. Not surprisingly he says, 'I bear on my body the brand-marks of Jesus.'

Three times he was beaten with rods, once he was stoned and left for dead, three times shipwrecked, including a night and a day in the storm-tossed seas, clinging for dear life to some piece of debris. Billy Graham jokingly said, 'When Paul entered a city he did not check up on a decent hotel, but first he examined what the jail was like—because that's where he expected to spend the night.' During his many journeys he was constantly in danger from robbers as well as the Gentiles and Jews who wanted to kill him. He endured many sleepless nights from exposure to the cold, damp night air because there was no home to welcome him. He writes:

> We are afflicted in every way, but not crushed; perplexed, but not despairing; persecuted, but not forsaken; struck down, but not destroyed; always carrying about in the body the dying of Jesus, that the life of Jesus also may be manifested in our body (2 Cor 4:8–10).

You would think that such uncommon valour would evoke the greatest response of love and admiration from those he served. Not at all; on the contrary, it is almost pathetic to hear this spiritual giant plead for recognition from the carnal Corinthians and then defend his ministry to the Thessalonians in 1 Thessalonians chapter 2. Finally, just prior to his martyr's death, he sadly remarks in a letter to Timothy, 'All who are in Asia turned away from me' (2 Tim 1:15). What a testimony of endurance!

In reading many biographies of great men and women of God, I have been impressed time and again that so many with outstanding ministries privately endured indescribable trials and afflictions.

W.F.P. Burton, whom I have mentioned, was a Congo pioneer missionary and prodigy of Smith Wigglesworth.

He once related to me how following an evangelistic meeting where many healings had taken place they returned to their shared bedroom and he saw Smith Wigglesworth pass what appeared to be a pint of blood from a kidney stone. It seems that perfected power comes from the Lord through his ordained gift of weakness. It is inevitable that we will be scandalised by negative events in our lives unless we understand that God will cause everything to work together for good as he conforms us to the image of his dear Son, Jesus.

God's crucible

The second time I visited India was with Arthur Wallis. I had waited with eager anticipation for the privilege of travelling with this esteemed man of God, who was also my hero. However, I was a bit overawed at having to preach and teach alongside him. During the first week of meetings we shared a bedroom. Each night after switching out the lights Arthur would turn my attention to the seminar I had taught and point out some error that had been made. One mistake was that the number of people in Elijah's time who had not bowed the knee to Baal was not 5,000 but 7,000.

I am ashamed to say I resented being told, I resented the late hour of day he corrected me and I resented listening to him snore while I wrestled with feelings of rejection. All in all, a rather pathetic response! Sunday morning came and Arthur preached.

As he continued through his sermon I couldn't help but notice that Arthur was now making the same mistakes in just about everything he had corrected in my preaching! It seemed like Satan was sitting beside me giving a nudge at each mistake. Lunchtime came and went; I was really down in the dumps.

Janette and the children were 5,000 miles away, I was tired and sweaty and I couldn't get out of my mind that

Arthur was guilty of making the same errors. After lunch I retired to my bedroom for the afternoon siesta but sleep eluded me. Finally I knelt by the bed and poured out my complaint to the Lord, concluding with, 'If this is the way it is going to be for the next five weeks I want to go home.' Suddenly the Lord spoke to me in the clearest way I have ever known. He said, 'What is that to you? You are in my crucible.' One word from the Lord and everything changed. 'Well, if it's you, Lord,' I sobbed, 'then it's all right.' The resentment just melted away.

It was my turn to speak at the evening meeting. I went to it a free man, washed emotionally, clean and clear spiritually, and preached with great conviction. That night as I jumped into bed cheerfully anticipating further correction, Arthur enthusiastically remarked, 'Do you know what, Barney? I think that's the best I've ever heard you preach.' I tried to thank him seriously but ended up having a good chuckle.

What price the Scriptures?

We love such passages as the thirteenth chapter of Corinthians. Many of us learnt it by heart at school. Behind this beautiful piece of God-breathed literature is a man's disappointed, hurting heart.

Paul was correcting the selfish, inconsiderate behaviour of the more affluent members of the Corinthian church. The *New Bible Commentary: Revised* makes these observations: 'In Paul's judgement the matter is serious,' 'he cannot commend actions which ruin Christian life and witness,' 'their manner is utterly selfish. They do not wait for latecomers (e.g. slaves) nor share what they have.' 'The Corinthians are despising both the dignity and the brotherhood of the church.'

Then consider Paul's memorable declaration to the Galatians:

I have been crucified with Christ; and it is no longer I who live, but Christ lives in me; and the life which I now live in the flesh I live by faith in the Son of God, who loved me, and delivered Himself up for me (Gal 2:20).

Sheer inspiration and revelation! Down through the centuries Bible teachers have expounded both in books and from the pulpit the marvellous truth of this verse. It was the inspiration for the much-read book *The Saving Life of Christ* by Major Ian Thomas. But a closer investigation of the situation behind this verse reveals that Paul is writing out of agony of soul. Listen to the pain in his words, 'You foolish Galatians, who has bewitched you?' (Gal 3:1), followed by, 'I fear for you that perhaps I have laboured over you in vain,' and again in chapter 4:19, 'My children, with whom I am again in labor until Christ is formed in you.'

In recent days I have found a fresh appreciation for the apostles Paul, James, Peter and John. The rich pearls of sound doctrine that unquestionably were inspired by God the Holy Spirit nonetheless were born out of the sandy irritation of disappointment and frustration which they experienced as false doctrine, false brethren and carnality invaded the fledgling church. We can go into almost any bookstore and for a relatively small price purchase a handsomely bound copy of the Bible. Maybe we need to pause and remember the price others have paid that we might have such free access to the Scriptures—too many paid with their lives.

Finally, let me close the chapter by honouring Joni Eareckson. What a beautiful example of life coming out of death! Hardly anyone would have ever heard of Joni Eareckson Tada if she had not broken her neck in a freak swimming accident and become quadraplegic. Her outstanding courage and dependence on Christ reach into and touch even the hardest of hearts. Many thousands of lives have been changed all over this world through her anointed ministry.

Remember next time you sit down to prepare that sermon or the phone rings for your attention late at night or yet again Mary wants prayer for her migraine headache, grace is free but not cheap. 'For you know the grace of our Lord Jesus Christ, that though He was rich, yet for your sake He became poor, that you through His poverty might become rich' (2 Cor 8:9). To lead God's people is a costly thing.

II

The Leader's Authority

'Poor government is better than no government.' So said Winston Churchill. The opposite to 'authority' is 'anarchy'. Probably the best definition of this word is found in Judges 21:25: 'In those days there was no king in Israel; everyone did what was right in his own eyes.'

Down through the centuries fierce debate has ensued over the type of authority that should be exercised. At times bitter conflict has broken out among rival factions. It has split churches time and again. For this reason care and sensitivity need to be taken in order that we don't repeat the hostilities of the past.

The Godhead

Egalitarianism is a curse. Satan ensnared Adam and Eve with the temptation 'You shall be as gods.' Contrary to what many claim, the Bible clearly supports 'hierarchy', beginning with the Godhead. There is no question that in the essential nature of deity, the Father the Son and the Holy Spirit are co-equal. It is plain to see that all three Persons of the Trinity are omnipotent, omniscient, omnipresent and eternal.

However, when it comes to function things are very different. For instance, Jesus said on one occasion, 'I do not speak on my own authority' (Jn 14:10, RSV), but what he heard, that he spoke. Speaking of the Holy Spirit, he said, 'Whom the Father will send in My name' (Jn 14:26). In this simple statement we find two expressions of authority: 'Whom the Father will send' and 'in My name'. Later Jesus went on to say, 'He,' speaking of the Holy Spirit, 'will not speak on his own authority, but whatever he hears that will he speak' (Jn 16:13, RSV).

We read in 1 Corinthians 15:24 and 28 that one day Jesus will deliver up the kingdom to his Father and himself be subject to his Father. Again in 1 Corinthians 11:3, we are told that 'God is the head of Christ.'

Angels and archangels

When it comes to the angelic realm we once again find different levels of government and function. For example, Michael in Daniel 10:13 is referred to as 'one of the chief princes'. The Bible speaks of cherubim and seraphim, clearly two separate ranks in God's heavenly host.

The church

The church is no different. In the plurality of leadership there is absolutely no equality of position anywhere in the government of God's people because it is impossible to function without authority.

Before anyone starts screaming abuse at me or ripping this page out, let me explain. If a church has elders it has hierarchy. If it has deacons, youth leaders, a Sunday school superintendent, senior steward, choirmaster, pastor, minister, or leading brother, these terms all reveal evidence of hierarchy.

Some Bible teachers in recent years have tried to tell us that biblical leadership is 'alongside', not 'over'. This position cannot possibly stand up when measured against 1 Thessalonians 5:12: 'But we request of you, brethren, that you appreciate those who diligently labor among you, and have charge over you in the Lord and give you instruction.' Hebrews 13:17 basically repeats the same thought, only this time with the added injunction to obey and submit to the leaders.

However, while the leader has the authority to be 'over', in practice his posture should be one of standing alongside. Paul could write to Philemon in verses 8 and 9, 'Though I have enough confidence in Christ to order you to do what is proper, yet for love's sake I rather appeal to you.'

Government is extremely important to God. It was he who established it in the Garden of Eden when he instructed both Adam and Eve to 'fill the earth, and subdue it; and rule over the fish of the sea and over the birds of the sky, and over every living thing that moves on the earth' (Gen 1:28).

It seems that God always operates in his dealings with mankind within the framework of covenant and government; it's the lamb and the lion, the priest and the king. We are the 'new covenant' people of God to whom has been given the kingdom of God. Jesus made this very clear in Matthew 21:43 when he said, 'The kingdom of God will be taken away from you, and be given to a nation producing the fruit of it.' Consequently we are called a royal priesthood.

Practical application

How does this affect us either as leaders or house group leaders? To start with, we need to bear in mind that God requires someone to be responsible (therefore accountable) for everything. It seems to me that there are two levels of government in the local church. First, that which oversees the whole, which we call 'elders', and then that which oversees the part, which we call 'leaders' forum' or 'deacons'.

I see the elders functioning in a similar manner to the Old Testament city elders who sat in the gate. The *Illustrated Bible Dictionary* (IVP) points out, 'The gates of the city, of which many have now been excavated such as Meggiddo, Hazor, Gezer, Tell Sheba, were the place of commerce and law, and here the judges sat to give their decision.' What came into the city and what went out had to pass by the government of that city.

The 'leaders' forum' is made up of people who have responsibility for a part of what goes on in the city, such as praise, the youth, the children, prayer, evangelism, pastoral care and the prophetic life of the community.

The 'elders' would normally meet weekly whereas the 'leaders' forum' would come together monthly or every six weeks. The benefit of this arrangement is that the 'elders' can concentrate on the major issues, such as serious pastoral problems, the vision and direction of the church, matters of church discipline, prayer and the word, and also the relationship with other churches.

The 'leaders' forum', including the presence of the 'elders', allows the senior leader to keep in touch once a month with all the leaders of the main sections of the church.

Each leader has his or her own subgroup of responsible people meeting with him or her at other suitable times, none of which requires the attendance of the senior leader himself.

Internal integrity and external integration

Charles Simpson, some years ago, coined the phrase 'internal integrity versus external integration'. He pointed out that everything healthy integrates with something larger, but at the same time keeps its own integrity.

In Basingstoke, it works something like this: the house group is part of a 'congregation', of which there are ten. These ten congregations make up Basingstoke Community Church, which is affiliated with the Evangelical Alliance. David Richards, together with myself, gives apostolic input to the church and is a member of an apostolic council of which I am the chairman. In recent years I have become a participant in a group of apostolic team leaders under the chairmanship of Gerald Coates that meets several times a year. I also attend annually a charismatic leaders' conference with about eighty other leaders. It has become a top priority to fit in with as many different Christian groups as possible.

Army or family?

The true nature of the church is family, not army. Though we are at war and are God's army yet we are not called to live in the army but in family. So Paul encourages Timothy to treat the older men as fathers; the older women as mothers; the younger men as brothers and the younger women as sisters. They are not to be treated as subordinates who can be ordered about, but as genuine family members to be handled with loving affection.

Spiritual authority is different from all other types of authority. It even transcends the most loving caring serving authority that could ever exist in the human family. That is probably why many Christians find it more attractive to spend time with their spiritual brothers and sisters than with their natural ones. Paul exemplifies it when he likens himself to a nursing mother. He also refers to Timothy as being his 'true son in the Lord'.

No function without recognition

Unless people recognise that God has given you to them as their leader, you cannot lead them. Neither can you exercise authority unless first of all they settle the issue in their hearts that God has given you authority concerning them.

You can bless them, encourage them, help them financially, but you cannot lead them.

A classic example is the account of Moses not being received by the Israelites. Luke records it for us in Acts 7:22–27:

> And Moses was educated in all the learning of the Egyptians, and he was a man of power in words and deeds. But when he was approaching the age of forty, it entered his mind to visit his brethren, the sons of Israel. And when he saw one of them being treated unjustly, he defended him and took vengeance for the oppressed by striking down the Egyptian.
>
> And he supposed that his brethren understood that God was granting them deliverance through him; but they did not understand.
>
> And on the following day he appeared to them as they were fighting together, and he tried to reconcile them in peace, saying, 'Men, you are brethren, why do you injure one another?'
>
> But the one who was injuring his neighbor pushed him away, saying, 'Who made you a ruler and judge over us?'

A good question! Who indeed.... God certainly had not! It was all a good idea in the mind of Moses.

Peter in 1 Peter 5:3 refers to 'those allotted to your charge'.

Paul defends his apostleship to the Corinthians in 1 Corinthians 9:2, saying, 'If to others I am not an apostle, at least I am to you.' Clearly there were some who did not receive him as an apostle.

My children, when they were young, used to play in a park not far from our house. Often there were as many as thirty other children, all congregating around the swings and slides. Suddenly, in the midst of their playing, my voice would boom out authoritatively, 'Come home at once children, it's teatime.' Only two responded to my voice because the others did not receive my authority.

Jesus, speaking of the shepherd's relationship with the

sheep and their acceptance of his leadership, makes the following observation in John 10:3–4:

1. The sheep hear his voice.
2. He calls his own sheep by name; signifying they were all personally known to the shepherd.
3. He leads them.
4. The sheep follow him.
5. They know his voice.

Jesus was never under pressure to add new people to his group of disciples. He could say in John 6:37, 'All that the Father gives Me shall come to Me.' He was under no inward compulsion to lower the price of admission to the rich young ruler, even though the Scriptures record 'He loved him.'

Both the leader and the led need to have a firm conviction in their hearts that God has joined them together.

Recently I received an invitation to a conference for pastors where one of the subjects being covered was 'How to break the 200 barrier'. Such terminology begs the questions: 'Two hundred from whom?' and 'Two hundred for what?'

If people are not being given by the Father, frustration and discouragement is inevitable.

Such language is nowhere to be found in the New Testament. Can you imagine Paul writing to the Ephesians on how to break the 200 barrier?

Both the leader and the led need to have a firm conviction in their hearts that God has joined them together.

Notwithstanding, let me add one word of caution to the issue of spiritual authority functioning only when it is recognised.

While I have special responsibility towards those whom God has allotted to my care, that charge cannot be allowed to prevent me from ministering to the needs of others. Less than an hour ago, while out walking in the beautiful countryside that surrounds our home, I came across a ewe flat on her back, struggling to get back up on her feet but without success. It was a pitiful sight. She was sprawling about in her own mess, with two little lambs trying to feed from her.

Now it is obvious that I was not the shepherd of that sheep. I had no authority to try to save her from certain death, but without giving it a second thought, I climbed over the fence and pulled the sheep back onto her feet. I was not successful the first time. It took several attempts before the ewe was able to remain standing in her own strength. What a relief! I felt deeply moved as I watched her slowly wander off followed by the two little lambs.

As I walked back to the fence, I believe God spoke to me. He reminded me that my responsibility was not exclusively to those who were part of my sphere but it included those who were his sick or injured sheep wherever I encountered them.

It seems, when it comes to acts of mercy, God is not precise. In Lamentations 3:22 Jeremiah declares, 'The Lord's lovingkindnesses indeed never cease, for His compassions never fail.'

May God help us to catch the passion of his heart toward the poor and afflicted.

The fruitful rod

The rod in the Bible is the symbol of authority. The choice of Aaron from among all the other leaders in Numbers 17 was determined by whose rod sprouted. Not only did Aaron's rod sprout, but it also put forth buds, produced blossoms, and bore ripe almonds.

If it is the true joining of the Lord, fruitfulness is bound to follow.

At the time when many of the disciples were leaving Jesus because of his offensive remarks concerning eating his flesh and drinking his blood, he turns to the Twelve and enquires of them, 'Will you also leave me?' to which

Peter replies, 'To whom shall we go? You have the words of eternal life' (Jn 6:68).

Wherever the Lord's grace is being extended, fruit is bound to follow. If it is indeed the joining of the Lord, the leader's words will generally bring life. I say 'generally' because it would be highly presumptuous for a leader to think that every time he spoke into a person's life it would carry the same inerrant quality as the utterances of Jesus, who could rightly declare, 'The words that I have spoken to you are spirit and are life' (Jn 6:63).

Spiritual authority cannot be enforced

Down through church history, whenever the church has tried to enforce Christocracy—that is, the rule of Christ—it has always misrepresented the Lord Jesus and usually ended up in disaster. A classic example is the Scottish Covenanter movement when it took up arms against the English for the cause of Christ. The motive was sound enough, it was the method that was totally wrong.

A few years ago a friend phoned me with a problem. He had spoken to his wife on three separate occasions about a particular matter that he thought was displeasing to the Lord. But it had made no difference to her. To quote him: 'It had gone through one ear and out the other.'

I immediately sent up one of my SOS prayers and felt I received some wisdom from above.

'Have you tried hitting her yet?' I enquired. The response was a stunned silence; then a little nervous laugh.

'Of course you can't do that,' I continued. 'You've done your part, now let God do his part.' There was a short pause, then he responded, 'Then that would be faith, wouldn't it?' 'Exactly!' I replied, adding, 'More-over, if she is wrong, God will deal with her, but by the same yardstick, if you happen to be wrong in your judgement of the matter, God will deal with you.' I could sense his morale rising as he said, 'Well I think I've got grace for that.'

God's instruction to young fearful Jeremiah was basically this: 'You speak what I show you and I'll be watching over my word to perform it.' In other words, Jeremiah was to do the speaking and God would take care of the doing.

One of my heroes (which is obvious from the number of times I mention him!), W.F.P. Burton, was greatly used of God in divine healing. Many people in Zaire, as well other parts of the world, experienced the healing power of God as this choice servant of the Lord anointed them with oil and prayed the prayer of faith.

Mr Burton's prayer of faith was unusual because of its brevity. He would put it something like this: 'Now Father, I'm doing my part, please do yours.'

The nature of spiritual authority is this: you cannot make it come to pass, only God can.

PART TWO

Practical Issues

12

Bereavement and Funerals

I was alone in my study, deep in thought preparing Sunday's message, when suddenly the telephone rang. Irritated at being interrupted, I picked up the receiver. 'Margaret Johnson here, sister in charge of casualty, Basingstoke Hospital.' Her voice sounded urgent. She continued, 'We have just had Mr and Mrs Chapman bring their little girl Sharon to emergency. She was unconscious on arrival. We did everything we could but I'm afraid she died.'

I could not believe what I was hearing. 'Did you say she died?'

'Yes, I'm sorry Mr Coombs, there was nothing we could do. I think the Chapmans would appreciate it if you could come to the hospital.'

'Yes of course,' I answered vacantly.

It was so difficult to accept. Lovely little Sharon—dead. She was only three years old. The last time I had seen her, she was sitting on her daddy's shoulders, legs wrapped round his neck, riding him like a pony.

By now my mind was completely numb. I felt bewildered and a little afraid as I drove speedily to the hospital. It seemed as if thousands of thoughts were all fighting for attention in my mind. What should I say? They had only been Christians five months. Would they blame God for her death? Would they become bitter? Would they even want to speak to me?

It was only two months previously that I had buried Matthew, their seventeen-day old baby. I recalled the chilling wind biting into my legs as we huddled together around the little white coffin being lowered into the ground. Now they were all alone; childless.

I arrived at the hospital and hurried into casualty. The sister seemed excited, 'Mr Coombs, we've managed to get Sharon's heart beating again. She's still unconscious but she may be all right.' She ushered me into a private room where Howard and Carol were waiting. Their faces displayed both fear and pain as they recounted the asthma attack and their desperate attempt to revive Sharon as they rushed to the hospital. They looked so forlorn and helpless. We prayed and committed little Sharon into God's loving hands. All night long the medical team fought for her life.

Howard and Carol waited anxiously in a hospital lounge. I found myself pacing back and forth in the hospital grounds pleading with God to preserve her life, every now and then glancing up at the room where I knew Sharon was lying helpless. The fact was she had suffered irreparable brain damage and soon after twelve noon the next day she went to be with Jesus.

Howard and Carol were exhausted. They stole away on their own and went for a long walk in the countryside. When they returned Howard put it this way: 'We went for a walk to find the end of the world so we could get off, but when we couldn't find it we came back.' Later on he wrote this very touching poem entitled 'After the Death of Sharon':

I dreamed of a walk we once walked together
in familiar surroundings
But somehow the paths we took
were new.
Our feet sought out a place to be alone

with our sorrow
Away from people who knew only death.

Unhurried steps.
In the dream we loved each other much
as we sought out solitude.
On the warm June afternoon
both of us lightheaded,
Laughing at times,
in a stunned silent way.
We knew that if we weren't gentle
with each other
we would break.

I asked you gently
'Can I say a word...I've
thought of something...
Can I say?
'Yes'

I spoke the word
and in the dream we stopped
in that strong new place
amid the familiar surroundings,
and at that word,
we gently cried and cried and cried
our hearts breaking together.

...we will awake!

That evening I took them to Maidstone in Kent, to Mr
and Mrs Geoff Mutimer who I knew would love and care
for them. As we drove along Carol fell asleep in Howard's
arms, which gave us the ideal opportunity to have a talk
man to man.

I remember it as if it was yesterday. 'If you want to
punch me on the nose,' I started, 'feel free, but I need to
say two things while Carol is asleep. What you have
experienced today has created a huge crater in your life.
You will either let Satan fill it with resentment that will
make you into a bitter person or you can let Jesus fill it
with his comfort and love and as a consequence give you a

ministry to others. The choice is yours. The second thing is this: the sooner Carol has another little bundle in her arms the better; this week would be a good time to do something about it.' Nine months later, Daniel Barnabas was born.

The following day Howard and Carol attended the Sunday meeting held in the Mutimer's home. Howard testified of God's comfort and care. The next day he testified to the gardener and helped him to receive Christ as his Saviour. It was clear that Howard was letting Jesus fill the hole with his comfort and love. They chose not to attend Sharon's funeral. I approved of their decision but with hindsight I think that this was a serious mistake. I will comment more about that later.

The need for a good cry

Every pastor sooner or later has to help people walk through devastating experiences like Howard and Carol's. Sometimes the people concerned are unknown to you but all too often it happens to people who have found a real place of affection in your heart; in which case it is so much easier to 'weep with those who weep'.

I had regularly visited Fred, a victim of Hodgkin's disease. A telephone call from the hospital requested that his wife visit as soon as possible because Fred was sinking fast.

I accompanied his wife and daughter to the ward but when we got there his bed was already empty. The ward sister drew us into her office and told us what we already knew. Both women began to cry freely. I took the daughter's hand while the ward sister put her arm around Fred's wife. I tried to comfort the daughter with, 'Now, now, don't cry,' and found myself being gently corrected by the ward sister. 'Don't do that, let her cry. She needs to let it all come out.' That day I learned an important lesson:

sorrow released is love expressed and is a powerful healing agent. It also relieves tension from pent-up feelings. I
have always found that a good cry is usually followed by
one's spirit being lifted.

While it is clearly necessary to concentrate on the resurrection and the blessed hope of eternal salvation (assum-
ing the deceased is a believer), my own experience of
losing a loved one is that some pastors so promote the
heavenly that you feel if you don't restrain the tears you
will be letting the side down. In fact, on one occasion, the
service was so victorious from beginning to end I felt
cheated of the opportunity of having a good cry which I
desperately needed. I am quite sure if I had been allowed
that opportunity I would have been far more receptive to
the wonderful assurance the pastor was seeking to give us.

The need for personal contact

There is no substitute for personal contact. John tele-
phoned me one night at 11.30 pm to tell me that Tim, one
of the men to whom he gave pastoral care, had just rung
him to say that his father had passed away that evening. I
asked John how Tim was taking it. 'Fine as far as I could
tell. I prayed with him over the phone and he seemed to
be all right.' 'John, that is not good enough,' I responded.
'You need to go round to his house and sit with them for a
while.' 'I didn't want to be a burden to them,' he defended
himself. 'Listen John, if they have taken the trouble to
phone you at 11.30 pm that should tell you how important
you are to them at this moment.' I added, 'They won't get
to bed till three or four in the morning.'

John was a good disciple. When I saw Tim later he still
could not get over the loving care of John. 'He not only
prayed with me over the phone,' he enthused, 'he actually
got out of bed, dressed, and came round and spent nearly
a whole hour with the family. They haven't stopped talk-

ing about it.' I silently smiled my approval with maybe just a tinge of carnal smugness.

It is always deeply appreciated when the pastor drops in for a short visit with the bereaved relatives after the service; only never stay too long, they need time together. Remember your presence will naturally inhibit their conversation. It is also wiser not to stay during the reading of the will.

The need to be careful what you say

I was greatly helped through a television programme on the subject of death and dying. Three people shared the things that hurt or disappointed them the most after the death of their partner. The first was that they felt they were a cause of embarrassment to friends. People seemed awkward around them, some stumbled over words, no one seemed willing to talk about their loved one. One person actually crossed the road to avoid a bereaved lady. As a result she found herself retreating into her thoughts, then she discovered people were worrying about her withdrawing into herself.

I still feel ashamed about my own failure with regard to Diane who had been delivered of a baby that had died in her womb. At that time the media was excited about the first man to the moon and back. When I visited Diane I talked about the latest news, trying to take her mind off her lost baby. She told me later how crushed she had felt.

The one person who could have helped her understand why, or who could have at least asked the right questions which would have released her to pour her heart out, had instead talked about the moon, the weather and the hospital food. My prayer at the end of the visit had seemed to her like a duty rather than a sharing of a burden before the throne of God. It was a lesson I would always remember.

I did not forget this important lesson when visiting my mother, six months after my father's death. The funeral had been a real comfort to her. All of us had gathered around in support, but time had passed and I suspected that few people talked with her about Dad any more, so I took her for a little drive. We parked the car and sat and talked for a while. 'Mum, I expect you're missing Dad a great deal aren't you?' The tears started to course down her face. 'We were married over fifty years you know. He was a good man.' She wiped her eyes and in a few moments was laughing away. 'You see I've had my hair permed.' 'Yes, it looks nice Mum.' She chuckled and then added impishly, 'Of course, your dad wouldn't have liked that.' It was clear that Mum had begun to make a new life for herself but she still needed an outlet for her grief.

The need to avoid trite answers and empty platitudes

Two things grieving relatives cannot abide are trite answers and empty platitudes. I shall never forget my mother's response to the minister after the funeral of my brother Tim. 'Well Mrs Coombs,' he said, 'one thing we can be sure of, Tim is with the Lord.' 'Yes,' replied my mother, 'but he's still my boy.' He missed it by a mile—all he needed to say was, 'Mrs Coombs, you're very much in our thoughts and prayers. I'll drop by in a few days' time and see how you're doing.'

The following is a list of trite remarks I have heard made by well-meaning people as they have tried to comfort those grieving:

It's all for the best.
My second marriage was much better than the first.
You're young enough to marry again.
You've still got other children, think of those who haven't.
You're still young enough to have more.
Jesus needed her in heaven.
He would have been a vegetable.
God may be trying to say something to you.

One incredible remark to a pastor whose wife was to be buried the following day came from a superspiritual woman who said, 'If you had faith, God would raise her from the dead.'

The need for dignity

Many well-meaning people think they are being a great help by taking over all the responsibilities for the bereaved. This is a serious mistake for two reasons: first, you take away a person's dignity when all they can do is sit there and watch helplessly while others make decisions and do everything for them. I served in the Metropolitan Police for ten years and one of our unpleasant duties was to knock on someone's door and inform them of the death of a loved one. A long-serving officer gave me this piece of helpful advice: 'After telling them the sad news and letting them have a good cry, see if you can get them to make you a cup of tea because it places you in need to them which results in giving them a sense of dignity.'

Second, you rob them of the therapeutic benefit derived from taking responsibility for their own lives. Having to make their own decisions is extremely beneficial for them; it keeps their minds occupied. However, there is one thing that is always a great help and that is transport. There are a number of journeys they have to make: registrar of deaths, insurance offices, the undertakers, the bank, the chapel of rest, the florist; someone to drive them to those places is usually much appreciated.

The need for a clear conclusion

Death is not only the ending of a life and a relationship, it also marks the beginning of a new life for the bereaved.

The saying 'Life must go on' expresses the reality of the situation. It may sound harsh but it is necessary. 'The king is dead: long live the king!' is a fact of life.

Abraham in Genesis 23:4 made this interesting statement after the death of Sarah, his wife: 'Give me a burial site among you, that I may bury my dead out of my sight.'

The burial ceremony is a very important experience for the bereaved. As the coffin is lowered into the ground, or is removed out of sight at the crematorium, it marks the end of an era. That is why I regret Howard and Carol's absence at the burial of little Sharon. It is the reason why I encourage even five-year-old children to be present at the funeral service so that they can experience their own goodbye. I used to have a certain technique when conducting funeral services at the crematorium. Usually there is a button nicely concealed in the pulpit which when pressed activates the conveyor belt or the curtain being drawn across. When it came to the moment of committal I would ask people to bow in prayer and after praying I would without pausing continue into the committal. When the committal was finished the people opened their eyes to find the coffin was now out of sight. I don't do that any more; I am convinced that my trying to make it easier for them was, in the long term, making it harder.

The funeral service

A helpful funeral service should have these three elements in it:

First, a recognition that their loved one has died. If it was sudden, such as a heart attack or car accident, the pastor could use such phrases as 'tragic loss' or 'sudden death' or 'shocking news' because that is how the family see it. If the death came after a long illness, phrases such as 'sad parting', 'long illness patiently borne', 'courageous battle' would be most appropriate and would accurately express the perspective of the family of the deceased.

Second, take time to honour their loved one. This should include a brief history of their life, their place of birth, their education, their wedding date, a record of any outstanding period of employment, the testimony of others and any acts of heroism or Christian service. All these help to make up a useful account of their life.

Third, turn the hearts of the bereaved towards the Lord Jesus to receive his comfort and peace at this sad time in their lives. When it is clear the dead person was a believer the pastor's job is so much easier. All the wonderful promises of eternal life, the resurrection and the riches of the ages to come are at your disposal. A minister's handbook for use at weddings and funerals will usually give you a good selection of relevant passages from the Scriptures. It is always nice to ask one of the relatives to do a Bible reading.

If the deceased was not a believer, you can still honour his life and achievements with integrity and take the opportunity to share with the mourners God's love for them and encourage them to ask God to come and comfort them in their hour of need.

But, you may ask, 'What about the committal at the graveside; doesn't it talk about God taking unto himself the soul of our dear brother/sister?' One doesn't have to stick rigidly to the handbook. On such occasions it is possible to say something like this: 'Trusting in the love and mercy of God we commit the body of our dear friend...to the ground, earth to earth, ashes to ashes,' adding any other suitable words that seem appropriate. The ceremony can be concluded by reciting the grace.

13

Preparing a Couple for Marriage

Next to receiving Christ, marriage has got to be the most significant decision a person can make. It is a binding contract between two people that joins together their possessions, their families and their income, as well as their bodies. It is a covenant made before witnesses. If the ceremony is a Christian one then the covenant is made before a minister and, most importantly, before God. Most often marriages produce offspring; what an awesome responsibility!

Stephen, our first child, arrived yelling a loud protest, having been dragged out onto planet earth (forceps delivery). As I carefully scrutinised this 7lb 12oz miracle of God's creation a dreadful sense of responsibility clutched hold of me. This was our doing; our son. A few moments of covenant pleasure produced a lifetime of increased love, joy, laughter, pride, mingled with anxiety, sleepless nights and tears.

As the wedding service handbook says, 'Marriage ought not to be entered upon lightly or unadvisedly, but thoughtfully and reverently, duly considering the reasons for which it was ordained.' Before taking the irrevocable step of making a covenant in order to be joined in marriage for life, it is important to have asked and answered some fundamental questions.

Unequal yoke

'Are they right for each other?' This is a delicate matter and needs to be handled sensitively.

Marrying a Christian with an unbeliever is, of course, out of the question, but what about a godly, dedicated young lady linking up with a carnal, half-hearted uncommitted Christian? What untold misery this can produce! Of course, the time to tackle the situation is not when they come to tell you they want to get married. The earlier it is faced the better.

Angela was my secretary, a bright, joyful, Spirit-filled Christian; also single. One day I heard through the church grapevine that she had gone out on a date with Philip, a young man more in love with motorcycles than with Jesus. The news left me feeling extremely troubled, so Angela and I had a serious chat. What were her aims in life? I knew she wanted to serve Jesus with an undivided heart. How, I asked, did she think Philip could help her fulfil those desires? I told her that if she was patient God would bring into her life a man destined to be a leader in the church. The situation was nipped in the bud—her heart had not yet got entwined with the heart of Philip. There were no more dates. Today Angela is happily married to Gary who pastors a church in one of England's largest cities. They have three children. Gary is helping her fulfil her dreams.

Some may call this heavy discipleship, others see it as simply 'being on guard for the flock of God'. Proverbs 27:23 puts it this way: 'Know well the condition of your flocks.' Hebrews 13:17 reminds us that our leaders keep watch over our souls and encourages us to submit to and obey them.

Infatuation can have an amazingly blinding effect. A thirty-five-year-old Christian man started to attend our Sunday services. Very soon he began to date an attractive divorcee who was a member of our congregation. She had come to Christ because of her marriage break-up and was apparently walking close to the Lord. Within a few weeks they announced their intention to get married. We asked them to wait six months until they got to know each other better. We then discovered he had already been divorced three times. The alarm bells began to ring loudly, so we asked for the names of the previous churches he had attended. We wanted to contact the pastors who could give us character references on his behalf. We also wanted to find out the reason for his divorces. He refused the information. The couple left our church, complained about our heavy-handedness to another evangelical pastor who married them almost immediately. Two weeks after the wedding, two of our ladies met the new wife in the street. Her face was badly bruised, one black eye and a split lip told the whole story. Now we understood why the man had been divorced three times.

The parents' blessing

When a couple come and share their decision to get married, the first question that should be asked is, 'Have you got your parents' blessing?' Our Western culture is saturated with a spirit of independence which almost certainly contributes a great deal to the enormous increase in divorce. By the way, God still hates divorce (Mt 19:3–9).

Dwight Alexander, a young American, was helping us with missionary work into Eastern Europe. Barbara Melville, a young lady in our congregation, caught his eye and his heart. Not only did he ask her father's permission to date his daughter, but he came and asked me as Barbara's pastor.

In fact, he asked me before Barbara had any idea that he was interested in her. As he showed that sort of responsibility, I was left in no doubt that Dwight would make an excellent husband for Barbara. They are today happily married and serving God in Hampton, Virginia, USA.

It seems that God pays special attention to whom a person's father happens to be. So we read, 'Saul the son of Kish', 'David the son of Jesse', 'Joshua the son of Nun'. Even in the New Testament we find 'Simon Bar Jonas', 'Bar' meaning 'son of'. The honouring of parents is a very big issue with God. In Africa great care is taken to include both sets of parents in the courtship procedure. Special visits are made on both sides in finalising the decision to get married. Sometimes these visits can last up to three days. We could well afford to have some of the African culture rub off on the Christian church.

It appears the church has become conformed to this world in the matter of dating, courtship and subsequent marriage. We should not be surprised, therefore, that divorce is rapidly increasing among Christians. In the USA the figures are almost equal to those of the unbelievers.

Long engagements spell trouble

Long engagements are not generally advisable for this reason. When a couple get engaged, they have in effect made a covenant to get married. This then produces a deeper sense of security, particularly in the young woman, which in turn increases sexual pressure. A line has been crossed, a hurdle jumped, a barrier removed; it's now safer to approach the final hurdle without actually jumping it. Unfortunately, all too often they make that irrevocable leap. The sex drive is the most powerful human force in a young couple. They are never so spiritual that they cannot fall.

The longer the engagement, the greater the intensity. When there is no release for this sexual tension then the couple encounter another problem, for nerves get frayed and arguments increase. Many couples complain they actually got on better before they were engaged. Four to six months is long enough to make all the wedding arrangements and prepare for their life together while at the same time keeping them fully occupied with little time for any hanky-panky!

Keep out of trouble

Paul exhorts Timothy in 2 Timothy 2:22, 'Flee from youthful lusts,' which means run away from them. It suggests strong decisive action, no lingering, no teasing, no chance of gradual enticement, but firm evasive counteraction. A courting couple need to agree on these safeguards. First, keep in groups as much as possible. Second, keep out of the back seats of cars that are parked in some secluded country lane or parking lot. Third, never babysit together—many a girl has lost her virginity while babysitting the pastor's children with her boyfriend. Fourth, if either one has his or her own private residence, then they should not spend time alone there together. Finally, praying together is a great antidote to temptation. Jesus told his disciples just before he went to the cross to 'pray lest you enter into temptation'. Any couple who, each time they went on a date, started by asking Jesus to be with them and to keep them from evil, would have a difficult job to wilfully sin against the Lord and each other.

Some leaders advocate increasing intimacy so that on the wedding night it is just one small step to go all the way. But I see that as encouragement to play with fire. A honeymoon is not designed so that on the wedding night the act of marriage is some fantastic emotional firework display. It is meant to be a time of tender, gentle discovery.

Practical arrangements for the wedding

Once it is clear that a couple are meant for each other and have received their parents' blessing, they should be taken through a basic checklist of all the things that need to be taken care of.

1. Date of the wedding. Is it convenient for the closest relatives? Easter and bank holiday weekends mean that guests who might have gone away for the long weekend now have their whole weekend tied up by a wedding, plus the potential problem of traffic snarl-ups.

2. Time of the wedding. If there are guests travelling a long distance by car and if the ceremony is too early, it means they have to get up at some unearthly hour. If, on the other hand, it is late in the day, they would get home in the early hours of the morning. That is all right if they are young, but if they are elderly then careful consideration needs to be taken.

3. Place of the wedding. Many in the so-called house church movement, having rejected the religious establishment, nonetheless are strongly attracted to their magnificent edifices to accommodate their wedding service. We're a funny lot, aren't we? If this is the case, the couple need to contact the vicar of that church as soon as possible and before any further arrangements concerning the date and time are finalised.

4. Registrar. It also needs to be ascertained whether a registrar is required. Many churches do not have a licensed registrar so the date and time of the wedding may have to be arranged according to the availability of the registrar.

5. Reception hall. A suitable place for the wedding reception often provides the biggest headache for the engaged couple. The sooner one is discovered and booked the better. Sometimes the size of the hall will determine whether the reception is a buffet meal or a sit-down affair.

6. Bridesmaids, best man and ushers. They not only need to be chosen and their help requested but it needs to be communicated clearly who will be paying for the bridesmaids dresses, plus small presents for each person participating in the wedding party.

7. Caterers. If the bride's parents are paying for the reception, then there needs to be clear communication between them and the bridegroom. Too often misunderstandings arise causing a strained atmosphere that can spoil what ought to be one of the happiest days of their lives.

8. Dresses and suits. It is surprising how long the major department stores require to make a wedding dress.

9. Florists. Once again, the sooner the florists are informed that their services are required for a certain date, the better.

10. Organist, musicians and singers. They not only need to be asked to participate, but music needs to be chosen so that they are well prepared and any fees agreed.

11. Photographer. Beware of amateurs. (Particularly police photographers, as they are used to photographing dead bodies or scenes of crimes and accidents! They are all willing to volunteer but they are likely to have the wedding party standing like a row of corpses. I know what I'm talking about, I've seen their morgue-like efforts.) Photographs record for ever what is one of the most important days of a couple's life. It's worth paying the price to have decent pictures taken that will be a treasure for ever. I have spoken to two couples whose houses burned to the ground, and in both cases one of the things that pained them the most was the loss of the family photographs.

12. Cars and chauffeurs. This is where a couple can save some unnecessary expense. Two or three good friends with nice cars suitably decorated for the occasion can quite easily provide adequate wedding transportation. I should have realised this before my daughter's wedding— I ended up paying for a Rolls Royce and a Bentley!

13. Guest list. The couple need to consult both sets of parents before finalising the list. Again, it is worth mentioning this is an area where serious misunderstanding can arise.

14. Master of ceremonies. Not all 'best men' make a good job of MC'ing the wedding reception, in fact, I have witnessed some positive disasters. The person chosen needs to be confident, with a warm personality. However, egotists need to be avoided. They can be an awful pain and embarrassment.

15. Future accommodation. Have the couple decided yet whether they are buying or renting? If they can possibly afford it, buying a home has got to be the best choice. When they are first married mortgage repayments may be more expensive than renting but within four or five years it will be less. Besides, they are building up equity. One couple I know decided to buy a house five years ago when the mortgage repayments were about $60 more than the cost of renting a home. Today, they have about $100,000 worth of equity and the cost of renting in their district is $300 above their current mortgage repayments. A short-term loss for a long-term gain.

16. Honeymoon. Some couples choose not to go away for their honeymoon. I think they make a serious mistake. They miss a glorious opportunity of spending unhurried time together. Properly planned, a honeymoon is not only a time of intimate discovery and sexual enjoyment, but a well-earned rest from all the rush and tear preceding the wedding day.

17. Parents. Finally, you may have to give some wise counsel on how to handle unacceptable demands of the bride or groom's mother or father. The quicker these are allowed to come to the surface and cleared out of the way the better.

Three months progress report and further counsel

The wedding preparation may require three, or as many as eight, counselling sessions. Having made sure all the wedding arrangements are taken care of there are now at least six questions the engaged couple need to discuss and answer.

1. Who is going to handle the bookkeeping? Not every man finds this responsibility easy. If the woman is better suited to this task there need be no reason why she should not serve her husband and the Lord in this way. However, it is most important that the husband understands that he retains the headship or government. He is the one who ultimately gives account to God for their stewardship of God's finance.

2. What are their expectations of each other? Matters like, who will be responsible for washing, ironing, cooking, gardening, painting, decorating, repairs, shopping, pressing trousers, polishing shoes, packing suitcases, washing up, preparing breakfast, early morning cup of tea, making the beds, driving the car, keeping it properly maintained, where they will spend Christmas—his or her parents? My wife's father was a do-it-yourself expert. Janette therefore expected that I would be just like him. Unfortunately I wasn't and she was most disappointed to discover I was generally ham-fisted when it came to trowel, chisel and hammer. Peaceful co-existence only arrived after Janette lowered her expectation and I raised my level of manly responsibility. I'm still trying!

3. What is their vision for each other and jointly for their marriage?

4. Are there any skeletons hidden in the cupboard, such as previous sexual activity, any sexual diseases contracted or abortions procured?

5. Have they discussed birth control, both the moral principle of it and, if agreed that it's right, then the method? Some methods raise serious moral questions.

6. If they had the choice, how many children would they like?

One month to go

There are still a few important matters to discuss and decisions to make:

1. Order of service

This needs to be finalised and arrangements made for its printing. It should include the words of the hymns or, if there will be a number of choruses, these can be printed on a separate sheet.

The names of those participating—the bridal parties, the musicians, the ushers, the person conducting the ceremony, should all be included. Remember, there will usually be a considerable number of guests who will feel total strangers apart from their friendship with bride or groom. The more information they have the warmer they will feel and the greater will be the success of the wedding.

2. Agape: the controlling principle in the act of marriage

Now is the time to talk about the 'act of marriage' (sexual intercourse). Naturally this is a very delicate matter, but the Bible points out some extremely serious principles which it would be irresponsible not to bring to the couple's attention.

I once read a book on marriage in which the author, to my mind, made a serious blunder. His proposition was this. We are made body, soul and spirit. In the Greek language there are at least three alternative words for love. *Eros* is sexual love and is the joining of bodies. *Phileo* is love expressed in companionship or friendship, the joining of souls. *Agape* love is the joining of spirits in spiritual communion.

He finalised his thoughts by saying, therefore, we *eros* each other physically, we *phileo* each other mentally/emotionally and we *agape* each other spiritually. I am convinced his conclusion is a misrepresentation of God's plan for marriage. Husbands are ordered by God to '*Agape* their wives as Christ *agape'd* the church and gave himself up for her.'

For a man, *agape* love is her good at his expense. It is sacrificial love. It is one-way love. It is unselfish. Paul in 1 Corinthians 13 says, 'It does not act unbecomingly; it does not seek its own.' *Agape* should permeate all three areas of the relationship. Janette and I have always enjoyed sexual fulfilment. However, during the first few years together I found, after making love, that I would feel an inward sense of emptiness. I could not understand it. It was almost like the feeling I get when I've watched an evening of television and go to bed dissatisfied. Then one day, while reading Ephesians 5:25, it dawned on me that when Janette and I made love, I was basically using her to satisfy my own sexual needs rather than making it my aim to bless her; I was failing to give myself up for her. Everything changed from that day. Jesus taught the measure you give is the measure you receive. What used to be 40 per cent satisfying pleasure, but with a clear post-intercourse dissatisfaction, now became closer to 100 per cent (it still gets better), with a spiritual understanding that what we had just enjoyed together was closer to how God planned it to be; therefore we were pleasing God. I always share this experience with a couple receiving pre-marriage counsel and include Paul's teaching in 1 Corinthians 7:4: 'The wife does not have authority over her own body, but the husband does; and likewise also the husband does not have authority over his own body, but the wife does.'

A good book to recommend is Tim and Bev LaHaye's book *The Act of Marriage* (Scripture Union). The couple should be encouraged to discuss it together and especially to take it with them on their honeymoon and read it to one another. It is amazing how quickly intimate communication dries up after the wedding vows have been exchanged.

Finally, the honeymoon is a wonderful time to experience unhurried tender discovery of each other. Secular books on the subject of human sexuality always seem to stress the importance of earth-shattering, volcanic-like orgasms. This wrong emphasis creates false expectations that very often seriously undermine the marriage from the start.

One last comment: the act of marriage is an act of covenant and is an intimate secret between them and nobody else. However, if, after many months, there seems to be some unresolved problem, I ensure that the couple know I am available for counsel.

14

The Wedding

Weddings are notorious opportunities for disaster to strike. I have experienced all types of weird, wonderful, hilarious, nail-biting catastrophes in my lifetime. Once, on one of the hottest summer days ever recorded, I waited patiently for over an hour for the bride to arrive. The poor organist gallantly soldiered on until, dripping with perspiration, his clothing visibly soaked, he finally succumbed to the heat and gave up.

The anxious, bewildered bridegroom nearly fainted with relief when his bride finally made it. Her limousine had been stuck in the middle of thousands of people who had gathered for a civic festivity. All the traffic was halted and all roads cut off until the procession had passed!

On another occasion I joined other guests in searching for the bridegroom's family who had been given the wrong location for the open-air wedding photographs to be taken. Having located the missing parents and safely deposited them with the photographer, I later discovered they had vanished again, making it obvious they were greatly displeased at being so humiliated.

The key to avoiding most wedding day calamities is careful planning implemented by good government. There are three individuals who, properly selected, can make all the difference: the minister conducting the wedding, the best man and the master of ceremonies in charge of the reception.

The minister's responsibility

Great care is needed in stage-managing the rehearsal. It is good to think sequentially. The proper conclusion of each segment of the service allows the next part to commence. For instance, just because the bride has appeared in the doorway of the church building it does not necessarily mean that she is now ready to proceed down the aisle. I have more than once listened to the bridal march played in its entirety, with the congregation having risen to their feet, but no appearance of the bride. Sometimes the hold-up is the photographer still taking photographs or sometimes one of the bridal party needs to make a last-minute emergency trip to the toilet. Arrangements need to be made with one of the ushers to give an indication that the bride and her entourage are perfectly lined up ready to proceed. Then a prearranged signal can be given to the organist for the ceremony to commence.

Bride's posture

It is all too easy for a bride and her escort to walk rather fast down the aisle. A good tip is for them to walk on their haunches and their heels rather than their toes. When a bride walks with the weight on the back of her body it naturally slows her down and causes her head to be held high and her shoulders back. She can then look around and smile at all the faces trained on her. It helps her to walk towards her bridegroom regally, like a queen.

Giving the hand in marriage

This is not a small, insignificant part of the ceremony. It is, in fact, the transfer of authority from the bride's father to her new husband. It adds significantly to the occasion for the father not only to give his daughter's hand to the bridegroom but to verbalise a blessing both to his daughter and to their marriage. Biblically, a father's blessing has powerful effect.

Finally, at the rehearsal, the bride and groom should be advised to eat a good breakfast on the day of the ceremony, or, if the wedding is in the afternoon, a good lunch. So much emotional energy is expended that many a bride or groom has been so tense they have felt weak at the knees. In fact, I have had two cases of fainting occur in the bridal party while the vows were being recited. It was most disconcerting to say the least. One final matter before we go on to the actual service. It is good that the bridegroom arrives thirty minutes before the service. This gives time for photographs, prayer and any wrinkles that may need ironing out.

The wedding service

There seems to be a growing trend for couples to be more flexible and innovative with the style of ceremony they desire. Extended praise and worship as well as dance is being given prominence, and for some the vows in the minister's handbook seem somewhat inadequate to properly express what is in their hearts. So they make up their own. However, it is worth bearing in mind that there are legal requirements that must be adhered to if the couple want to avoid the embarrassment of having to return after their honeymoon and repeat their vows once again.

It's also worth checking over the vows they plan to exchange to each other. I have heard some strange ones over the years; some have been extravagantly mushy, others seem to have nothing at all to do with their impending life together. One fellow promised his bride he would seek first the government of God, not only in his marriage, but in his city, his county, his nation and the whole world. With promises like that one would get the impression he was a member of parliament, or in the diplomatic corps. Not at all! He was a shop assistant with no chance of ever being promoted beyond the position he was holding at the time.

Sensitivity

Care also needs to be taken in how far the Christians exercise their freedom to worship and praise the Lord the way they are accustomed to on a Sunday. Remember, usually quite a number of relatives are there because they wish to honour the couple getting married and in their own way give them their blessing. Anything that makes them feel embarrassed and out of place is undesirable. I know of one wedding where one bridesmaid, who also happened to be bride's sister, was so offended she stormed out of the building in a raging temper, quickly followed by the rest of her family. Hardly the ideal way for the newly weds to start their life together!

Elders' blessing

It is very special when, after all the usual ceremony is completed, the elders gather round and pray God's blessing on the marriage with the laying on of hands. It is also an ideal time for prophetic words to be spoken over them. If it is suitable, the parents of both bride and groom could be included in joining with the elders in giving their blessing.

The best man

The main responsibility of the best man is to make sure all the practical arrangements on the day run smoothly: vehicles, airline tickets, the rings, that the photographer knows what he can and what he cannot do; also to help organise the prompt availability of guests and family who are to be included in the photographs.

It is his job to draw up a list of all those the bride and groom desire to be photographed and then to notify them when and where the pictures will be taken. He needs to ensure the photographer takes only the time that has been apportioned to him and no more. At almost every wedding reception I have ever attended the bridal party have been late for the reception and each time the photographer has been to blame.

The master of ceremonies

So many carefully planned receptions have been thoroughly spoiled all because the MC allowed the proceedings to drag on. He needs to have a well prepared programme that is meticulously tailored to the wishes of the newly weds. It is their special occasion, not an opportunity for him to show off his unrestrained egotistical personality. His comments need at all times to be honouring. Part of his job is to focus the attention of the guests on the couple and their family. He needs to have a pleasing disposition and exercise enough authority to keep things moving along without being overbearing. He should be able to project his voice so that everyone in the room can hear him—many a wedding reception is spoiled because of the incoherent mumblings of the speakers.

It would be extremely helpful for those planning to get married if their pastor were able to hand them right at the beginning a set of printed notes setting out counsel and information similar to that which I have shared in this chapter.

15

Baptisms

Some years ago, a well-known American Bible teacher related the following story. Every year a certain Pentecostal church conducted a mega baptismal service. All the new converts from the previous twelve months were baptised on the same night. It was the church's highlight of the year. The building was always packed to overflowing.

The church auditorium was of unusual construction. The choir stalls rose almost perpendicularly behind the platform and pulpit, instead of the usual terraced style. The exquisite see-through glass baptistry was also situated on the platform at the base of the stalls. This was most convenient because on the baptismal night the giant curtains that for the previous twelve months had hung decoratively at the sides of the choir stalls were now pulled across, which made each stall into a changing room for those being baptised.

On this particular evening there was an extraordinary air of expectation. A quiet hush fell on the crowd as the first person descended into the waters. She weighed in at about 300lbs. The slightly-built pastor was clearly uneasy as he watched the water rise significantly the further she stepped down. It did not help matters when she nervously enquired, 'Do you think you can manage?' She clung to his arm terrified as he intoned, 'I baptise you in the name of the Father and of the Son and of the Holy Ghost.'

Now it is a well known fact that overweight people are extremely bouyant in water. Whether she thought he was trying to drown her, we are not told. Without doubt his extra effort at putting her under caused her to panic. She in turn struggled to get her head back up above the water, at the same time dragging the pastor down and under so that she was now on top of him. The congregation sat and watched this life-and-death struggle with wide-eyed amazement. To be trapped in a small glass tank underneath a 300lb lady must have been the pastor's worst nightmare come true! It is beyond explanation how a frail, puny man, when faced with certain death, can summon up superhuman strength in order to survive; but it happened, for this gallant leader once again found himself on top. The poor woman now went quite berserk; as she reached up to grab something to lever herself into a standing position her hand discovered the hem of the giant curtain. With one mighty effort the whole curtain broke loose from the ceiling and came crashing down.

The situation was rapidly getting worse, for suddenly all the changing rooms were exposed to the astonished congregation! Dozens of people were in various stages of undress. They scurried to hide behind chairs or grabbed any available item of clothing to cover themselves.

The star attraction was an older gentleman who suffered from both deafness and short-sightedness. Here he was on his hands and knees completely naked except for one sock, trying to find his spectacles which had fallen on the floor, the added complication being that his hearing aid was fixed into the frame of the spectacles.

The pastor by now was exceedingly anxious to recover the situation, so he called for all the lights to be turned out and for everybody to get dressed. Unfortunately our elderly friend with the one sock was oblivious of all the fuss. He was quite unaware that he had become a star overnight; neither had he heard the command to get dressed. Fifteen minutes later the pastor ordered the lights to be restored, only for the now bewildered audience to be greeted with the rear end of our unintentional entertainer—still clothed with only one sock, still on all fours, struggling to locate his lost glasses!

As you see, baptisms can go dreadfully wrong. This chapter is designed to give a few pointers and helpful hints to ensure that the spiritual significance of the experience is not spoiled by lack of preparation, inappropriate behaviour or avoidable mistakes.

You will also have gathered by now that when I use the word 'baptism' I am referring to believers' baptism by immersion. Almost all of the new churches hold to this theological conviction, and this book is mainly addressed to such people.

Confession to the lordship of Jesus

Believers' baptism is the public confession that one has been crucified with Christ at Calvary, is now dead and is being buried with Christ in the waters of baptism, and is raised to newness of life up out of the waters. It is a confession that our sins have been washed away and that we have been delivered out of the kingdom of darkness and transferred into the kingdom of God's dear Son: that Jesus Christ is now Lord.

Therefore it is extremely important that the person being baptised both believes and understands these facts and that he or she can, with utmost sincerity, confess that the risen Lord Jesus is now his or her Lord and Saviour.

The moment they can affirm this with understanding and conviction they are ready and qualified to be baptised. Apart from needing time to prepare the baptistry, there can be no biblical reason for anyone to be kept waiting. The sooner the better!

During the sixties and seventies controversy centred on

baptising in the name of Jesus; in fact, some people got re-baptised because they had only been baptised in the triune name. Personally I could not, and still cannot see what all the fuss was about. However, I began to use the following words: 'I baptise you into the Lord Jesus in the name of the Father and of the Son and of the Holy Spirit. Amen.'

Practical tips

First of all, make sure the tank has been properly drained from its previous use. There is nothing worse than having your head stuck under stale musty-smelling water. How do I know? That's what happened to me! Then fill it up to about 3 feet. Anything less can give the person baptising severe back injury. Be careful about filling the baptistry too full. The displacement that takes place when putting a person under, especially if they are rather large or if you could lose a few pounds yourself, can cause the tank to overflow.

If you choose to wear waders beware because the water can rise above the top and fill them up! This once happened to the late Jamie Buckingham and he ended up having to remove his waders and leave the baptistry in his underpants, simply because he didn't have the strength to lift his feet up the baptistry steps.

Next, make sure the immersion heater is switched on early enough for the water to be comfortably warm, but ensure that it is not too hot—you do not want a cardiac arrest in the pool. I've seen people emerge looking like boiled lobsters; in fact, on one occasion we had to pour in about twenty buckets of cold water and then we only managed to bring the temperature down a fraction. They were fairly cooking that night!

Now to the actual baptism. Do not, like so many, stand in the middle. Aim to set the candidate about 2 feet from one end and then pull him down into the water toward the opposite end. The only exception to this would be if you

baptise either an elderly person or someone physically
handicapped, when it would be safer to just push their
head forward and under the water. Bath stickers might be
helpful to show where one needs to stand. The reason for
all this counsel is there have been too many cracked
skulls. You may have noticed at some baptisms a man
standing dripping wet with a strange glazed look in his
eyes. He hasn't momentarily swooned in the Spirit, he's
actually suffering from severe concussion—the pastor has
just smacked his head against the hard tiled wall!

Two people, one standing on each side of the candidate, is the ideal number, and if they stand about 1 foot
behind the candidate then they will be pulling him or her
toward them. Doing it this way is not such a strain on the
lower back.

Now to the question of appropriate dress. In recent
years it is not uncommon for women to wear jeans when
being baptised. However, this has not always been welcomed, especially by older folks who were accustomed to
seeing both men and women clad completely in white.
The problem is that white dresses and blouses once
soaked in water can be very revealing as well as clinging;
hardly the perfect expression of seemliness.

If white dresses and blouses must be worn, advise that a
swimsuit be worn under the dress plus a few lead weights
sewn into the hem. Also have an attendant waiting with a
large bath towel to wrap around the woman as she climbs
up out of the baptistry. Otherwise there is no reason why
jeans should not be worn, unless we particularly want to
appear traditionally 'angelic'. It is clearly evident that on
the Day of Pentecost the fledgling church did not stay up
all night sewing together 3,000 baptismal garments for the
new converts! It did not seem to bother God then, why
should we think it would bother him now?

Of course, two separate changing rooms are required.
Both need to be comfortably heated, especially in winter.

Hot tea, coffee or chocolate kept ready in flasks is particularly welcomed.

Finally, time needs to be given either prior to baptism or after for prophecy or Bible readings to be spoken over each person. I recommend they are given afterwards, so there is no sense of spiritual vacuum immediately after the baptism. It is also an ideal time to lay hands on the candidates' heads and pray for them to be filled with the Holy Spirit. Another important consideration is the giving of a new name. It may happen that the new convert was originally given a name that honoured either Satan or some other satanic dignitary. With their consent and co-operation, it is the ideal time to change it.

This procedure frequently occurs in Third World countries. It is worth giving some careful thought to the matter here in the West. The baptismal statement could go something like this: 'Because of your confession that Jesus Christ has become your Lord and Saviour I baptise you with the new name "John" into the Lord Jesus in the name of the Father and of the Son Jesus and of the Holy Spirit. Amen!'

16

Cells for Life

The last thirty years or more has witnessed an amazing phenomenon called the charismatic movement. In 1949 it was reckoned there were 7 million Pentecostals and charismatics in the world, but by 1989 this figure had mushroomed to 352 million. Much has been made of the practice of charismata (the gifts of the Holy Spirit), but probably the most prominent feature of this renewal has been the proliferation of home/cell groups.

Ron Trudinger, in his superb little book *Cells for Life* first published in 1979, added these words on the front cover: 'Home groups: God's strategy for church growth.' This has turned out to be astonishingly accurate. In the book he mentions the Full Gospel Central Church in Seoul, South Korea, having a membership of 45,000 people. Only thirteen years later it has grown to over 700,000, with the whole membership carefully divided up into small groups.

Other nations have also seen a dramatic increase of small groups. Many, if not most, of our churches have some sort of cellular structure where people meet midweek for Bible study and prayer in a warm atmosphere of caring fellowship. In recent years, however, there appears to be some decline in the enthusiasm of those participating. I would like to try in this chapter to offer some thoughts that might help in some small way to redress this trend.

Training

Any businessmen reading this book would heartily agree with the following statement: 'If I were to run my business in the same mediocre manner in which the church is run, I would be bankrupt in no time at all.'

Few churches known to me give any sort of training to house group leaders. Seldom is any clear vision imparted, neither are leaders equipped on how to lead a meeting, nor on how to draw out the shy and the nervous so that they feel comfortable and safe enough to participate. Communication skills are not taught. In many instances the groups are led by novices or recent transferees from other churches, the latter being a potential recipe for disaster. If Ron Trudinger's words 'Home groups: God's strategy for church growth' are the truth, then senior leaders in the church ought to be giving this matter urgent attention.

The churches with which I am closely linked have commenced an annual seven-day training conference entitled 'Cells for Life' in the hope that some life and vigour may be restored to many cells. Everything necessary should be done to eradicate boredom, apathy and monotonous predictability. Vision, strategy and adventure need to be restored. Of one thing you can be certain: the disciples were never bored under the leadership of Jesus. The same could be said of those who accompanied the apostle Paul. Jesus pointed out to Nicodemus in John 3:8: 'The wind blows where it wishes and you hear the sound of it, but you do not know where it comes from and where it is going; so is everyone who is born of the Spirit.'

God is extravagant, creative, and in many ways, surprisingly unpredictable. Our cell groups ought to reflect these aspects of God's nature. The following seven reasons for the existence of house groups were first established in Basingstoke back in 1969. This is the substance of the vision we believe God gave to us in the early days of the charismatic movement. Nothing has changed my conviction since then.

1. House groups provide a place for meaningful fellowship. In preparing foundations for our church life, we state clearly that we believe the body of Christ is essentially relational. It is not possible in a Sunday morning meeting to achieve any sort of quality interaction among the church family. In most congregations, all the people see is the pastor's face and the back of each other's heads. Outside the building after the service, little conversations may break out such as:

'How are you doing?'
'Oh fine, fine.'
'Well, good, good. How's your mother?'
'Well, not so good, she's still a bit poorly.'
'Oh, I'm sorry to hear that. Well, I need to be going. Isn't it good to have fellowship together? 'Bye for now.'

Fifteen people meeting regularly on a weekly basis have an excellent opportunity to develop genuine relationships. The type of relationships I have in mind are those which have integrity and are able to cope with confrontation. Someone once said, 'You cannot drive a 10-ton lorry over a 3-plywood bridge.' For people to truly walk in the light with each other, a strong bridge of trust has to be established. It is only as we walk in the light that unhindered fellowship is able to exist.

2. House groups provide a place for everyone to be cared for properly. It is impossible for a pastor or the church office to care adequately for all the pastoral needs of a congregation. Every member is enjoined in Galatians 6:5 to bear one another's burdens. It is all too easy for the sick, the unemployed, the bereaved, the poor and the single parents to be inadvertently forgotten. The bigger the congregation, the greater the danger. One lady I met while visiting one of our members in hospital had been there for over three weeks, having undergone major surgery, without receiving one visit from her minister. Her pain was only compounded further by her observation of the daily visits our church member received from the other members of her house group, as well as the twice weekly visits from our pastoral team.

Pastors don't have the time to cook meals and store them in the freezer or wash and iron clothes, vacuum and clean the house, babysit, collect the kids from school, paint and decorate the house, fix the plumbing, mow the lawn, weed the garden, repair the fence and a host of other chores that need attending to when someone is hospitalised, or finds himself or herself immobilised. Over the past twenty-five years I have heard hundreds of fabulous testimonies of how God wonderfully provided for someone in desperate need through the loving care expressed by the other members of their house group. One pregnant mother with two children was confined to bed for the last three months of her pregnancy. During that time the house was kept spotless, the children were taken to and collected from school, all the family's clothes were washed and ironed and meals were carefully prepared and frozen to be easily defrosted and heated by Dad when he returned home from work. That is love in action! And that is fulfilling the law of Christ.

3. House groups provide a place where everyone can function properly. In Ephesians 4:16 we read that the body of Christ grows through every joint (relationship) with which it is supplied when each part is working properly. In 1 Corinthians 14:26 Paul writes, 'What is the outcome then, brethren? When you assemble, each one has a psalm, has a teaching, has a revelation, has a tongue, has an interpretation. Let all things be done for edification.' It is not possible in a congregation of over fifty people for everyone to participate in the fashion of 1 Corinthians 14:26. But it is uniquely possible in a house group.

4. House groups provide the ideal setting for Christians to celebrate the Lord's Table in a more intimate and relational way; something I believe to be thoroughly biblical. When I was in the early days of pastoral leadership at Basingstoke, the usual *modus operandi* for conducting Holy Communion was that on the first Sunday in the month the morning service was extended by fifteen minutes. Then, on the third Sunday in the month, the evening service was extended by twenty-five minutes. This longer extension meant we had enough time to sing two whole hymns, though they needed to be short ones!

The service was quite formal. The bread was sliced up into small squares and the wine (blackcurrant juice) was service in little glass cups. I cannot say I looked forward to these times. In fact, on each occasion I found myself having a struggle with my conscience. The problem was having to say the words, 'And after supper he took the cup.' A little voice inside my head would ask the question: 'What supper?' A piece of bread half the size of a lump of sugar could hardly be called supper.

Two years later I was invited with my wife and family to Greece to speak at a Youth With A Mission conference. On our second Sunday there we lunched at one of the local restaurants. Our attention was drawn to the increased activity of the waiters as they began preparing a large table for about twenty people. The aroma from the kitchen was fantastic. Soon the party arrived. We concluded the group was made up of Grandad and Grandma, four more couples and their children. After a while the waiters returned with a succulent, roasted lamb, heavily garnished with exotic herbs and spices, which rested on a king-size platter. Placed in front of Grandad was a long large loaf; we watched with intense fascination as the old man took the load and, standing up, began to ask a blessing. When he had finished, he began to break off sizeable pieces of bread and then distributed them to each person one by one until all were served. Suddenly my eyes were opened! He was doing what was called in Acts 20:7 'breaking bread'. It was a complete meal that was served on the night of the Passover. It was a full meal that Jesus used to inaugurate the New Covenant meal, and it was a real meal, albeit a simple one that the Corinthian believers ate at their love feast in 1 Corinthians 11. Paul would hardly have corrected them for gorging themselves on tiny cubes of bread and getting tipsy on wine served up in tiny thimble-sized glasses!

I am aware my liturgical friends will see this differently, but I concur with Gordon D. Fee's position in his excellent commentary on First Corinthians (published by Eerdmans) in which he argues that the Lord's Table was a part of a real meal. Now I don't want to offend my readers unnecessarily but I find myself asking the question: 'How on earth did we arrive at the present style of Communion service?' Surely it ought to be as it was in the early church, recorded for us in Acts 2:46: 'Breaking bread from house to house' (or, 'in the various private homes').

A letter from Pliny the proconsul of Bithynia in AD 110 to Trajan the Roman emperor gives us this helpful insight into how the early church met together: 'The Christians were accustomed to meet on a particular day before dawn and to sing an antiphonal hymn to Christ as though to a god.' They also, says Pliny, bound themselves by an oath (*sacramento*) to abstain from crime and to behave honestly. By this the baptismal oath is evidently meant, which Pliny, not unnaturally, misunderstood, considering that it was administered not once but frequently to the same persons. After this the assembly broke up and did not meet again till the evening, when they partook of a common meal, apparently the Christian *Agape* (*The History of the Christian Church to AD 461* by F.J. Foakes Jackson, published by George Allen and Unwin Ltd).

It seems that the early church fathers were concerned about the abuse that had infiltrated the *agape* feast and decided to separate the Eucharist from the full meal. This decision may well have contributed to a decline of relational fellowship that was replaced by increasing sacramentalism and liturgical institutionalism. Special people were dressed in religious clothes, using special language, meeting in distinctive buildings. Instead of seeing themselves as 'the church' they started going to church. Out went the priesthood of all believers or, as Peter puts it, 'a royal priesthood'. In came the professional clergy. This, I'm sure, appears to some to be rather simplistic and it may not be exactly why it all changed, but it seems to me a real possibility.

Down through the history of the church there appears to have been from time to time a return to the simple expression of the church meeting in the home and to the celebration of the love feast in small groups. I believe we are experiencing once again another of those particular times. I have not only participated in the Lord's Supper in homes, but in restaurants, hotels and school halls. One very moving experience occurred in Czechoslovakia. Let me tell you about it. Together with another Englishman, I was enjoying a delightful meal with a lovely old couple. The husband had spent six years in prison for his faith in the Lord Jesus. Halfway through the meal the old man looked across the table straight into my eyes; I could see tears were beginning to form and I knew he was saying, 'Let's break bread together.' Using the bread that remained on the table and ordinary water for wine we remembered the Lord Jesus in his death. The Holy Spirit's presence filled that little room. Our tears flowed together as we sang, each in our own tongue:

Oh, the love that drew salvation's plan!
Oh, the grace that brought it down to man!
Oh, the mighty gulf that God did span at Calvary!
Mercy there was great, and grace was free;
Pardon there was multiplied to me;
There my burdened soul found liberty, at Calvary.

We had to sing very quietly because a member of the dreaded secret police lived in the next-door apartment. I couldn't help thinking at the time that this is what Jesus had in mind when at the Last Supper he said, 'Do this in remembrance of Me.'

5. The house group should be an evangelistic base. In the following chapter is a testimony written by David and Maureen Church who now lead the Milton Keynes Covenant Fellowship. It gives an exciting account of what can happen when a group of believers who live in a given locality commit themselves to pray and believe for their neighbours to be won to Christ.

6. Participation in a house group quickly reveals anyone who has unique gifts in teaching or leadership. I often wonder what happens to potentially gifted leaders in mega churches that do not have a small group structure. People with outstanding talent can sit there undiscovered and vegetating for years, resulting in them feeling frustrated and bored. Such people can often be viewed as rebels and troublemakers, when all they need is a piece of the action.

7. Variety is the spice of life! On the other hand predictability is a guaranteed method of strangling the life out of house fellowship gatherings. Doing the same thing week after week soon becomes boring and uninviting. At the same time it is so easy to fall into the trap of thinking all house group leaders are creative and innovative. The fact is they are not. With this in mind and with the help of Ron Trudinger's book *Cells for Life* I have compiled the following twenty-six suggestions in the hope that if your group has gone to sleep, or worse still, has actually died, these ideas may help you to wake it up or resurrect the thing back to life! In any case I trust you will find them helpful and inspiring:

(a) Have a Bible study or series of Bible studies led by one of the senior leaders or a guest speaker from another church. Members should be encouraged to take notes as well as ask questions.

(b) Have another house fellowship come and take your meeting for you. These evenings can be wonderfully stimulating.

(c) Get yourselves invited to another house group to take their evening for them. The more people who participate the better. Such an evening can be exciting and challenging. It needs to be well prepared. Testimonies, poetry, teaching a new song, giving a brief teaching, leading or closing in prayer are all ways the group can take part. This is not the occasion for the leader to hog the show. It is sufficient for him or her to introduce the group and let the members get on with it.

(d) Invite a worship leader to come and lead an evening of praise and worship. This can include learning some new songs plus some training in four-part harmony. Without wishing to encourage irreverence, you can be assured the evening will not pass off without extended periods of uncontrolled hilarity as well as priceless times of praise and adoration.

(e) Prepare a planned question-and-answer session to expand on Bible teaching given the previous Sunday. The group leader needs to be careful that it is the message that is being chewed over and not the messenger!

(f) An evening of special prayer for specific needs, such as healing, which could include anointing with oil and the laying on of hands. This is also an ideal setting to pray for some new church venture, or an unpleasant challenge the church or an individual is facing.

(g) Hold an up-to-date testimony evening; this is particularly appropriate at the year's end. Make sure it is a current testimony and not one that has been dug out of the archives. Each participant needs to be informed beforehand.

(h) Invite a member of the group to give his or her life story. The account needs to include at least two painful episodes as well as two deeply satisfying and fulfilling incidents. If the person sharing is willing, an opportunity could be given for the rest of the group to ask questions. This needs to be handled extremely sensitively. You could make this a monthly event until all the members have taken their turn in the hot seat.

(i) Hold a Bible quiz. This makes for a first-class fun evening, but remember to include some easy questions for those who are new Christians.

(j) Plan a meal together, including Communion. These occasions provide a unique opportunity for people to confess wrongs and to ask for forgiveness. The closer a group comes together, the more likely is the necessity for such honesty and vulnerability.

(k) Write letters to missionaries. But what could be even more interesting as well as fun for the missionary would be the recording of personal messages. The sound of laughter and banter would make the listener feel they were part of the evening.

(l) Enjoy a musical evening of records and tapes, where six or seven people select their favourite piece and explain why it is special, a little along the lines of *Desert Island Discs*. This should be well planned and prepared.

(m) Prepare a craft evening. Have everyone working and learning together; something new but not too difficult, eg, simple pottery or painting.

(n) Hold a carefully planned games evening with perhaps the special aim of learning more about one another. The games should be easy to play so that no one is made to look foolish.

(o) Enjoy a weekend retreat together. It ought to be as informal and relaxed as possible. As much as you're able, do everything together. If folk go off doing their own thing it defeats the purpose of the weekend.

(p) Plan an evening to prepare for special outreach, such as carol singing or a dramatic presentation in a local hall, with an evangelistic emphasis.

(q) The outreach itself. Sometimes it is good to join forces with another house group from the same locality in order to swell the numbers and improve the quality of presentation.

(r) While the operation of the gifts of the Spirit should be often in evidence at meetings, it is a good idea to have an occasional evening when these are specifically explained and encouraged.

(s) Have a writing evening. Don't necessarily inform people beforehand. Distribute paper and pencils and urge each person to express themselves freely. What they write can be in the form of prose, prayer, poetry or praise. You will be quite surprised with the quality of creativity. However, remember to tell them that poetry does not necessarily have to rhyme or contain rhythm.

(t) Go out for a social time together. Skittles, boating, walking, skating, swimming or, in the late spring and summer, a barbecue. This is an excellent opportunity for inviting non-Christian friends and neighbours to join you. It allows them to see that you are not a bunch of stuffy old religious kill-joys but are quite normal and natural and know how to enjoy some good, clean fun together.

(u) Hold an appreciation night. This is when each person has to sit and listen to the others tell what they most appreciate about that person, especially where there is clear evidence of God's grace operating in some exceptional way.

(v) Invite everyone to a book evening—led by a Christian bookshop manager or salesperson—with lots of good books.

(w) Plan a special missionary night—with either a visiting speaker, missionary video or tape. If the speaker has come from outside the local scene, then not only should they be given an honorarium but also their travelling expenses.

(x) Lend-a-helping-hand day. This is where the house group select a number of needy people, such as the elderly, the physically handicapped or those who are incapacitated. Having with due sensitivity discovered previously what would be of the greatest help, then go about meeting that need without fanfare or drawing attention to oneself. If there is any difficulty in finding suitable candidates to help, the social services would be only too willing to give you some names and addresses.

(y) Prepare an evangelistic prayer evening. This is when a list is drawn up of non-Christian neighbours and friends and against their names a few details are noted, such as the names of their children, if appropriate, and any current tensions in their lives like marriage problems, financial stress, unemployment, sickness or bereavement. Then each person is lovingly prayed for. Quite often, as the group are praying, the Lord will reveal one or more people who are in need of a more extended time of prayer. Care ought to be taken not to treat these names like a shopping list to be rushed through as quickly as possible. They are people for whom Christ died and are therefore of great value to him.

(z) Invite someone from the public services such as a doctor, a policeman, a nurse, a local politician, a lawyer, a fireman, or an ambulance attendant, to share their testimony and explain how their faith helps them in their job. This would be an ideal occasion to extend an invitation to non-Christians.

Let me conclude with two more things. The first is this: you do not have to start each meeting with 'praise and worship'. In fact, if you find yourself without a musician and your group is rather small, not to mention including two or three people who are tone deaf, then have a round of prayed 'thank-you's' instead.

Second, if you have a fun evening and you invite non-Christians, don't go getting all religious at the end and feel you must close with a 'word of prayer'. I think the Lord must get pretty exasperated with the way so many of us repel sinners with our liturgical fixations.

Having made that point, I would not like to finish this chapter without encouraging you to get the saints into the Scriptures as much as possible. All the above suggestions have their place, but they should never take the place of regular times in the word of God. Just as sand needs to be mixed with cement to create a good bond, so these twenty-six suggestions and others need to be added to good Bible teaching for the same result. Fifty-fifty would seem to me to strike a good balance. May God give you wisdom.

17

Cells for Growth

The house group should be an evangelistic base. The following testimony is from David and Maureen Church, who lead the Milton Keynes Covenant Fellowship. It gives an exciting account of what can happen when a group of believers who live in a given locality commit themselves to pray and believe for their neighbours to be won to Christ. David writes:

'Often during the late sixties I would retire to the toilets at the Swindon engineering company where I worked and pray, "Lord, please get me out of here."

'Maureen and I were praying for a new environment in which to live with our three children, Andrea, Stephen and Shaaron, when in July of 1968 I nonchalantly picked up an engineering magazine and flicked through the pages without any real intent. There it was before my very eyes: a vacancy in Basingstoke for a "job right up my street"! I immediately applied for the position and got it.

'Right up my street also was the local Baptist church, which was undergoing considerable transition. Its pastor, Barney Coombs, had received the baptism in the Holy Spirit, and consequently new dimensions of praise and worship and church life were taking place in the congregation. These were heady days, and to complete the package we discovered a house that was in the process of being built; it was nearly completed. It was the first of fifteen being built in the fields of what only a few weeks before had been nursery gardens.

'By May of 1969 my "toilet prayer" had been well and truly answered. I had been working in the town since the September of the previous year but now the three important pillars of work, church and house were all in place. Number 2, Frithmead Close stood like a sentinel at the entrance to a half crescent of houses which were under construction, with a playing field at the end of it.

'On evenings and weekends of this beautiful summer you would have seen us with our children playing hide-and-seek in the houses under construction, so that by early winter we had visited every room of each house. Often we wondered who would be our friends and neighbours but we also left a secret in each one upon its completion. We had stood in every living room and prayed, "Lord, as you have brought us here, so bless those whom you will bring here also!" It was as if our house stood at the entrance to all God would allow into Frithmead Close.

'The following February a lovely family from Hove in Sussex came house-hunting in Basingstoke. They were told the Baptist minister was a retired policeman. Knocking on his door for advice, they expected to see a sixty-year-old man. However, to their surprise, the door was answered by a petite wife and a six-foot-four-inch husband who were both in their early thirties. He had not retired but had resigned in order to pursue the call of God! They were told, "Why not try the Harrow Way estate. There is a couple there called David and Maureen Church who are praying over bricks and mortar and asking God to send them living stones.'

'May 21st was the moving in day for Chris, Jenny and their three children. It also happened to be the anniversary of when we had taken up residence in the close. Here was our first anniversary present of answered prayer! More than a friendship sprang to life that spring day; God began to knit our hearts together. The years that followed were exciting as well as demanding, but each challenge only served to prove that God had indeed made us a joint in the body of Christ. When it became time for us to leave for Milton Keynes, it was necessary for us to leave our youngest daughter behind to finish her education. We never had a second thought in making our decision; it was obvious that the right place for her to say was with Chris and Jenny. It was home from home!

'Our daily family interactions became full of both happy and tearful memories that grew from learning to trust each other with many intimacies of life. One memorable evening we covenanted together that Thursday supper time would be a regular time of praying for our close and immediate neighbourhood. Whatever the weather or time of the year, whenever nine o'clock arrived, we put down our tools and affairs of life and gathered together for prayer. On some occasions it was not unusual to have a bath early on a winter's evening and be seen running up and down the close for supper and prayer in our pyjamas, dressing gown and slippers (all done decently and in order). But oh how we would cry out to God for his blessing—nothing would deter us.

'We were sowing for a harvest not yet seen but one we were convinced would eventually arrive! Some Thursday evenings instead of staying in the house and praying we started prayer walking around our neighbourhood. At the same time we began to adopt a posture of prayer on behalf of our neighbours. Whenever we left our homes for local shopping, taking the children to school or visiting other people, we would pray for the occupants of each house as we walked by so that an incredible spiritual awareness of the people of our neighbourhood gradually came upon us. The people were the same as they were before but, where once there had been a dim recognition of houses, front gardens and fences, now there was a vital interest in the folk themselves, with a growing sensitivity to their needs.

Now, when we prayed for them corporately, there was a frequent chord of agreement as to what we felt the Holy Spirit was showing us regarding their circumstances. In fact, we wondered at times how we could ever have been so blind about all the needy folk in our neighbourhood. The whole place seemed to be full of sad, anxious and disillusioned people! No longer were we walking around with our head down and occasionally giving a furtive glance toward our neighbours' houses, but rather, we began extending the love of God to them by the gleam in our eye and smile on our faces—all intermingled with pleasant comments and words of encouragement. Our shoulders were thrown back and our heads erect through the excitement due to the change in our attitude. We were Christ's ambassadors and were affecting the spiritual atmosphere of those around us.

'On the opposite side of the road, halfway down the crescent, a little family moved in that had sadness written all over them. The lady was so downcast she could hardly lift her head or smile, while her husband used to drive his car past our house with the posture of an undertaker. Immediately opposite us, however, lived a happy family without a care in the world—at least that was how it seemed. Their three children were age to age the same as ours and many were the pranks they got up to. There was a well trodden pathway between our two houses as our families exchanged life together. I well remember an early experience, when their car refused to start, of daring to pray over the open bonnet and the engine exploding into life at the next turn of the ignition key. My prayer frightened myself and amazed the husband, "Cor b----- 'ell," he exclaimed, "p'raps there is a god!"

'Our younger children were in the same class as each other but one day their boy wandered away from the comparative safety of the close on to a main road and straight into the path of an oncoming car; the driver had no chance. The car struck him before the driver could get his foot on the brake, leaving him lying in a crumpled heap. Some time later the telephone rang at home with a very distraught father sobbing, "Dave please come quickly. He's hurt real bad!" As long as I live I will never forget those words. Taking it in turns, my wife and I did not leave the hospital's intensive care unit for four days. All the time his little life was ebbing away, until finally he died.

'But in the little lad's death, something else was being born in the close.

'Life for us was totally disrupted by this sad event. Evening after evening we sat across the road with the grieving parents and Maureen often stayed the whole night, which meant Chris and Jenny looking after our home and children while we spent time with our neighbours. During this time Chris and I redecorated their whole kitchen, working from early evening and on throughout the night. The whole close had attended the funeral with great affection and sympathy, but within only a few days most of them had returned to their daily routine save for the fact that many were left pondering the question: "Who were these families that stopped what they were doing, took on each other's responsibilities, shared their cars, did the shopping for one another and cut each other's grass?"

'Not long after this tragic event there was a knock at our front door and standing there was Annie, the sad lady from the mid-point of the crescent. "I hope you don't mind," she said to Maureen, "but I've been watching you people for some weeks! I should have been the one able to help that couple because I lost a child in a cot death. That's the reason why we moved here, in order to start life again, but I can't even go upstairs and look in the bedroom when her sister is asleep for fear of the worst. Sometimes, I have to even phone my husband and bring him home during his working day, just to look into the cot. How do you manage it?" Sitting down with a cup of tea Maureen began to explain. "Annie, the answer is not with myself; it's with the Lord Jesus."

'The following Monday morning Annie found herself praying, "Please Lord Jesus, come into my life and help me. I can't go on much longer or I will die!" Jesus did just that! The change in her began immediately. She had been on such heavy dosages of Valium that there were times when she neither knew the time of day nor the day itself. Within a week all the need for any medication ceased. The following Monday she found herself going around the house singing a song she had learned during her first Sunday at church! Laurie, her husband, was happily confused by it all and was heard to remark, "Even better than the girl was when we were courting!"

'Thursday night prayer was now going full swing, especially with the addition of Annie. Three months later, Laurie received Christ and was thoroughly born again in our garage—he only came over for a bit of wood! Also within this time-span Annie's widowed Mum gave her life to the Lord.

'I can still hear the clang of the playing field gate as on some occasions we would have supper and then move out into the field to pray. There were seven of us now, for such was the interweaving of life that the oldest child, Paula, got saved on the day of her young brother's funeral. She soon became an important part of the youth group that gathered in our home and where she eventually found her husband. Like mushrooms popping up, so Christians were now appearing in the neighbourhood. Every time a house was put up for sale we would pray that God would send the purchasers of his choice and then drop a little letter of welcome upon their arrival. At the end of our first year of praying we had grown from two to four, then to eight, finally ending the year with twenty-five!

'One of these was a young man who lived close to the playing field. On hearing that he was off to university we began to target some Thursday night prayer for his salvation; we also included his parents. During his first term away, I was intercepted by his rather officious mother as I was about to take my daily walk to work across the playing field. She was concerned over a letter she had just received from her son at university in which he informed her that he had got himself saved. Did I think it was all right!? My reply was, of course, very positive, to which she said, "Does that make him the same as you people around here?" "Yes, very much so," I responded. "Well," she continued, "then it can't be too bad, can it?" He soon became a choice part of our spiritual family and eventually married one of the young ladies in our church.

'There is neither the time nor the space to relate all the stories of those who contributed over the years to our growing numbers. However, one lady deserves special mention.

'Edith Lamble moved into our area at the age of seventy-four following the death of her husband and the sudden death of her only son. She was now all on her own and feeling desperately lonely but she wanted privacy to spend Christmas with her own thoughts. Something strange and wonderful happened to her during this time. The only way to describe it is that the Lord Jesus suddenly became very real to her. Some weeks later, I was endeavouring to explain the way of salvation when she interrupted me and said, "Oh, you mean what happened between me and Jesus on Christmas day!" Edith was baptised shortly afterwards and filled with the Holy Spirit. Soon her home became a major centre of attraction for both young and old. Shortly before her death, she described the last ten years as the best of her life, with which many of us concurred.

'The neighbourhood by now had many and varied cross-reference points which were impossible to keep up with. But a definite expression of "having all things in common" was now emerging.

'We considered our house as an "open home" and felt it to be a prudent way of using our resources to bring others into all the beautiful aspects of Christian family life as enabled by God's grace. The only difficulty was that our normal-sized three bedroom house was full with our own children. By the kindness of Edith Lamble we purchased a large caravan as sleeping quarters adjacent to the house. "Young men for the kingdom" was our motto! We tended to recruit and then redistribute them later on, but some of the young men stuck to us as our "sons" as well as becoming true brothers to our own children. None more so than Andrew Forbes, Trevor Clift and Robbie Frawley, who all became indivisible from our own. Andrew later moved across the road to Laurie and Annie's home where, because of having a young family, they fixed a 10.30 pm curfew! This proved to be unacceptable for a twenty-year-old so a regular system was devised between him and our son Stephen whereby Andrew would go upstairs to bed and straight out of the back bedroom window by ladder. Little did we know that one day he would become the husband of our youngest daughter Shaaron who at that particular time was still attending school. However, this lad along with Stephen and Mark Coombs, Julian Sayers and our son Stephen had tremendous pulling power upon the youth of our area. Our youth group started with one boy and seven girls; three years later it had grown to forty-eight fellows and forty-five girls. Our home was the regular Sunday night after-church venue. Many youngsters were drawn in from the immediate vicinity and some parents began asking whether their teenagers could be invited along and come under the wholesome influence of these "clean live-ers". To see 100 young people happily competing on a Friday night in "our" playing field was a credible evidence to many of the local populace of the positive effect of the kingdom of God! And so we continued to grow.

'There was a progressive, positive change taking place;

it was one that you could almost taste. Most people were no longer going around with their heads down as happens in some streets, but were actively waving and chatting to each other. So much so that on one occasion a Christian family commenced cutting the front lawn of an unwell non-Christian family. It was not many minutes before another non-Christian joined in, followed by another, then many others. Because there were too many people for the amount of work available in one garden, they moved as an army from one garden to the next until six were completed—all interlaced, of course, with cups of tea, biscuits and good banter! The point is, no one organised it, but the spiritual environment allowed it!

'Encouraged by this, on another occasion we organised a street tug-of-war competition, odd numbers versus the evens, to be fought in the playing field. I still have photographs of that afternoon when each husband, wife and child spread themselves out along the rope for the best of five pulls. On another occasion, each family produced a simple side-show on their front lawn—each one different—of darts, skittles, and hoopla. It was agreed that when the 2.00 pm blast of the whistle sounded from the mid-point of the close, each family would emerge and compete for the Champion Family Award. What an afternoon and evening that was! Through the initiative of the Christians there was a furthering of an harmonious, gregarious community spirit such as it is rare to experience. But all the while the Thursday night prayer time was continuing.

'Prayer numbers were steadily increasing, and as the ripples in the pond spread to adjacent streets we had East Indian Catholics and restricted Plymouth Brethren joining us. The latter found it hard to accept many of the "environment friendly" things but could not deny the influence of the power of God that was occurring. Christmas became an obvious contact point for a neighbourhood event, but not only for mince pies and sausage rolls. These evenings were a regular feature year after year. Trading on the relationships deliberately fostered in many and varied ways during the previous seasons, we grew more daring in our friendly approach. Normally it would be unthinkable to hear of the stereotype bank manager, personnel manager, chain store manager, headmaster, civil servant, ships merchandiser, electrical foreman, toolmaker, accountant, student, financial director, each with his wife, taking it in turns to sing a carol or read the Scriptures! The aloofness, image presentation and reputation of the professional business person would not allow such things to happen, but they did; every year! A miracle was taking place.

'On one such occasion, the manager of an extremely well known chain store confided to me personally of his own faith in Jesus. But I knew that it was a faith well smothered by religious influence. He also said he would do anything for his wife to have a love for Jesus "like ours". On to the prayer and action list she went, the action being to understand her as a friend more than we did already, until one evening, on a night out with "the girls", she prayed the sinner's prayer and received Christ in a shop doorway! How undignified—a chain store manager's wife getting saved in a shop doorway—but when a person is ready, God will meet him or her anywhere! Another problem was that it was impossible for her to conceive, try as they had over many years. This was a very private, personal matter to her but on getting born again her sense of identity, trust and confidence so overcame her shyness and insecurity she asked for prayer and advice about the situation. The dangerous step was the question of her having an operation. This could have a long-term, adverse effect upon her health. After prayer, and by God's grace, faith replaced the fear that had been resident in both of them, to the point of enabling them to say, "We are just going to trust God for the outcome"—a complete reversal of belief had taken place, and they now have three lovely children and without any side-effects or health problems whatsoever. Although promotion has moved them on to other towns since then, they have remained good, true friends ever since. All the time God was continuing to add Christians to our neighbourhood as we shall see.

'I remember one evening in 1974 when I retired to my bedroom to pray. My wife and I so loved the close and its people that this was not an unusual occurrence for either of us. On this particular early evening I lay prostrate on the pastel green carpet. Although I knew I was in the room yet in a strange way I wasn't! I was above the houses at the mid-point of the crescent and was able to see all the residents. All I can say is that God was with me saying, "I too am looking down and this is yours to care for!" That same evening I physically stood upon that same spot and prayed out loud before walking both pavements and others besides. The event had tremendous impact upon many of us for somehow it not only gave confirmation and approval to what we were doing but also impetus to make it work without strain or striving—God was giving us his backing!

'Our community life together was reaching up other roads too and a joining of hearts for the larger area was also taking place. Where once there had been no Christians, or silent obscure ones, now they were springing to life and popping up all over the place. The area was coming alive with Christianity. We were genuinely proving that by consistent calling on God you can move people in and out so that you change the character of the populace with regard to the volume of people and the spiritual atmosphere. Every house up for sale was a prayer target for God to move into it the people of his choice.

'We discovered that to pray correctly for or against a situation it was important to have as much practical information as possible. Therefore, each Thursday, all who attended would bring their jigsaw piece of information and fit it into or add it on to what we already knew. You would be surprised at the compendium of neighbourhood knowledge that accrues to the spiritually discerning with a love for their estate! It is not nosiness, or prying, but the information and discernment that God allows to be given in a multitude of ways and circumstances over a period of time to those who wish to carry spiritual government and authority on his behalf. We know that in prayer we held up moves as well as released them and that marriages and families at a point of fracture were repaired. We also discovered that women walking in the Spirit of God were more sensitive in discernment than men. Nearly every time a house, person or situation was laid upon our hearts for intercession, details would come to light later that confirmed in a remarkable way the accuracy of what had been discerned. God was with us doing immeasurably more than all we asked or thought according to his power at work within us!

'One house just around the corner became vacant, and to this situation we applied prayer. Our praying was that we would receive occupants who would blend in comfortably both to bless and be blessed, adding to the freedom of the neighbourhood. On returning from work one day, my eldest daughter described a man who had visited our house during the afternoon armed with my name and carrying a briefcase. He seemed for all the world like a double glazing salesman and for some reason I was annoyed and ready to send him away should he bother to return as he had promised. Well he did return; to tell us he was going to purchase the house we had been praying over! He was the newly appointed headmaster of a local school and they were Christians looking for fellowship. Peter, Ruth and family well complemented the rest of us. They had been praying in another town while we were praying in ours. God then brought us together for the further strengthening of our area; their children well matched ours in fun and adventure. Their arrival meant that ten of seventeen houses in the immediate vicinity had Christians in them and so the snowball of influence rolled on collecting others on the way. Starting from the day of just one family on the corner, there were eventually fifty-three Christian adults and thirty-nine children within a three-minute walking distance. These formed the nucleus of a new church plant in south Basingstoke.

'Sad days also occurred, however; days that drew us closer together. A couple with two young girls got saved. But tragedy struck within a few months when Peter discovered he was terminally ill. He never did see his third child for he died of leukaemia shortly before his baby son was born.

'The years 1969 to 1982 were golden ones indeed; also foundational, for little did we realise then that God was going to plant us out into Milton Keynes. We were praying that the God who grows a frail youth into 100, who turns a home into a community and into a church is again using his expansive skill among us in Milton Keynes.'

It is over ten years since David and Maureen Church, together with twenty-six others, moved to Milton Keynes. During that time they have worked and prayed to such an extent that they have been able to plant three other churches. David and Maureen work under the correct assumption that Jesus meant what he said when he stated, 'The Son of Man is come to seek and to save the lost.' It is unthinkable for them to either lead a house group or a church without reaching out to their neighbours or friends with a view of winning them for Christ.

As the Father has sent Me, I also send you (Jn 20:21).

18

Teaching the Scriptures

I always feel disappointment when I hear a pastor of Christian leader say, 'Well I'm not really theological.'

Sad to say, it is a statement all too frequently made by leaders in the charismatic movement as well as leaders of the new churches. The truth is, we ought to be theological; in fact, every believer ought to be theological, not just those who study at a theological college.

If we want to see those entrusted to our care growing strong, spiritually prosperous and fruitful, able to withstand the debilitating influence of daily life, then we will make sure they are like the trees mentioned in Psalm 1 that are planted by the river of water whose roots reach down deep into the water of God's word. To use another analogy, a good shepherd makes the flock lie down in green pasures and leads them beside still waters.

When I was at the Metropolitan Police Training College at Hendon, I was taught 'Your authority is in knowing.' It is exactly the same for a Christian leader. Knowing and understanding the Scriptures is a vital part of the heart and substance of our leadership. That is why it is so important to hold the Bible in a high place. If we dilute its accuracy and authenticity we actually undermine our own spiritual authority, for without the Scriptures we have no real godly authority.

The preparation and presentation of a teaching should be viewed as hard work. I once heard of a bishop who used to go to his study wearing boots in order to remind himself to work hard at preparing his sermons!

The following are twenty-four points to consider what have been helpful to me when preparing and presenting a message. None of them is original. I have learned them over the years from a variety of sources.

1. Discover it! It is most important that we find out what the Lord wants us to teach. To come up with our own good ideas is to eat from the tree of knowledge of good and evil, thus committing the sin of presumption. Of course, as often happens, it is the Lord who takes the initiative in placing his burden in our hearts. It seems he likes to surprise us by choosing unusual times and unexpected places in which to do it. Bob Mumford, a well-known Bible teacher from the USA, was sitting in his car parked at the side of the road when he noticed an empty Coke can lying discarded on the grass verge. God chose this moment to say to him, 'My people treat my leaders the same way. They drink the contents then discard the vessel through whom I chose to bring those contents to them.'

If we are having difficulty in coming up with a message, it may be the Lord is saying that someone else ought to be giving the teaching.

2. Water it! Next, we need to pray that the Lord would open our eyes to unlock the spirit of the verse or passage. When we pray like this we are not leaning to our own understanding but we are truly acknowledging the Lord. In fact, it is an act of humility. The Lord has promised to give grace to the humble; so in faith we can expect an answer.

3. Survey it! We need to become thoroughly familiar

with the passage or verse. The best way to do this is to read it repeatedly in your usual Bible followed by several readings in other translations.

4. Research it! We are abundantly blessed with many aids to help us in this task. Bible handbooks, commentaries, Bible dictionaries and word studies all help us to answer questions such as:

(a) Who wrote it and to whom was it written?

(b) When was it written? The answer could have a significant bearing on your whole presentation. For instance, some Bible scholars believe the First Epistle of Peter was written between AD 64 and 67. This was a period of intense persecution against the church, with the situation about to become even more horrific. If this is accurate, then it boldly underlines many of the statements of Peter, such as 'tested by fire', 'fiery ordeal' and 'sharing the sufferings of Christ'.

(c) Where was it written from? Some of Paul's letters were written in prison, which makes a number of his comments rather more poignant.

(d) Why was it written? What was the occasion or situation that caused the letter to be written? For example, at Corinth there existed a strong party spirit among the members. Gross immorality was also being tolerated. There was an abuse of the Lord's Supper as well as a misuse of the gifts of the Holy Spirit, and some did not believe in the resurrection. All these and a few other matters are carefully addressed by Paul.

(e) What social, commercial, geographical or historical data can we find that may have a bearing on the writing? The letters to the seven churches in the book of Revelation are a perfect example of how the writer uses local knowledge to set alongside some spiritual truth. Take for example Revelation 3:18:

I advise you to buy from Me gold refined by fire, that you may become rich, and white garments, that you may clothe yourself, and that the shame of your nakedness may not be revealed; and eyesalve to anoint your eyes, that you may see.

Halley's Bible Handbook informs us that Laodicea was a banking centre proud of its wealth, that it was noted for its manufacture of rich garments of black glossy wool, and that it had a medical school that made powder for treatment of eye troubles. Such information greatly helps the presentation to come alive.

(f) How was it written? This question may not seem to have too much importance. But some Bible critics have tried to make much out of the difference of writing styles that exists between First and Second Peter. In 1 Peter 5:12 Peter tells us, 'through Silvanus, our faithful brother...I have written to you briefly.' Obviously, Silvanus presented Peter's thoughts in a way that is more grammatically correct than that evident in his Second Epistle.

5. Summarise it! It is most important to discover the overall thrust. This is made that much easier if you can find out the key verse or even the key word. In John's Gospel the key verse is John 20:31: 'These have been written that you may believe that Jesus is the Christ, the Son of God; and that believing you may have life in His name.' It now becomes clear why John gives us seven representative miracles and the famous seven 'I am's'. The first four verses of Luke's Gospel make it very clear what Luke is endeavouring to do. He concludes in verse 4 by saying, 'So that you might know the exact truth about the things you have been taught.'

6. Dissect it! It now needs breaking down into main points that are manageable. This is how I divided Philippians 3:1–10.

1. Three things to beware of (v 2):
   (a) Dogs
   (b) Evil workers
   (c) False circumcision

2. Two characteristics of true circumcision (v 3):
   (a) Worship in the Spirit
   (b) Glory in Christ Jesus

3. Six aspects of Paul's self-righteousness (vv 4–6):
   (a) Circumcised an Israelite
   (b) Of the tribe of Benjamin
   (c) A Hebrew of the Hebrews
   (d) As to the Law a Pharisee
   (e) A zealot
   (f) Blameless as to the Law

4. Two issues Paul settled as loss (vv 7–8):
   (a) All religious things
   (b) All natural things

5. Two types of righteousness (v 9):
   (a) My own righteousness
   (b) The righteousness that is through faith in Christ

6. Four things Paul wanted to experience (v 10):
   (a) To know him
   (b) The power of his resurrection
   (c) The fellowship of his sufferings
   (d) Being conformed to his death

7. Don't try to make it mean now what it never meant then! I borrowed this line from Gordon D. Fee and Douglas Stuart's excellent book entitled *How to Read the Bible for All It's Worth* (published by Scripture Union). Every home group leader should read it. One of the most common errors made in home group Bible studies is to read a passage and then ask the question: 'What does it mean to us now?' Until the group has discovered what it meant at the time of writing, it cannot find out what it means now. I am not saying that God cannot speak to someone in a special way through a verse out of context, but we must

realise this is not the proper meaning of that verse. God called me out of the police force to serve him as a pastor as I was reading Isaiah 52:11–12:

> Depart, depart, go out from there, touch nothing unclean; go out of the midst of her, purify yourselves, you who carry the vessels of the Lord. But you will not go out in haste, nor will you go as fugitives; for the Lord will go before you, and the God of Israel will be your rear guard.

I had returned home late that night having arrested someone. Janette had already gone to bed. I was quietly enjoying a plate of cornflakes and drinking a cup of coffee while reading my Bible. Suddenly these two verses hit me. Without a doubt I knew it was the Lord. I was on holy ground. Instantly I found myself kneeling on the floor and shaking all over as I told God if he would help me I would do his will. The point I am making is this: as powerful an experience as this was, I cannot now make a doctrine out of that encounter from those two verses.

8. Don't read into the passage what isn't there! It is important to understand what is explicit; in other words, that which is plainly stated. One example of an explicit saying is John 14:6: 'I am the way, and the truth, and the life; no one comes to the Father, but through Me.' Compared to that is one which is implicit, as found in 1 Timothy 5:17: 'Let the elders who rule well be considered worthy of double honor, especially those who work hard at preaching and teaching.' This verse not only states explicitly that elders who rule well should be worthy of receiving extra pay but that very statement implies that the elders who do not rule well should receive less income than those who do.

9. Examine it in context! Make sure you examine each verse or passage in its context as well as checking it with a commentary. It will save you many embarrassments. For instance, the verse 'A man's gift makes room for him' (Prov 18:16) does not mean 'a person's charismatic gift or ministry will make room for him or her'; it simply means it is an inducement or present. Again, many preachers use Philippians 4:13—'I can do all things through Him who strengthens me'—to imply that it means literally everything and anything; however, the context shows the verse is strictly limited to Paul's physical and economic well-being or lack of it. How many times have you heard a preacher use Revelation 3:20 as an evangelistic message to unregenerate sinners when the context shows Jesus was sending a letter to the church at Laodicea?

One of the worst mistakes I know of was a young man preaching on John the Baptist. He told his congregation that not much was known about John's father Zacharias in the New Testament; however, much more was revealed about him in the Old Testament in the book of Zachariah the prophet, as they were one and the same person! The fact that at least 400 years separated the two men seemed not to have occurred to him.

10. Prepare thoroughly! Always research and prepare more material than you will use. When you have a strong grasp of your subject it greatly helps you to deliver your message with increased confidence. Your bucket of water is coming from a larger reservoir so that when people ask you questions concerning the teaching you have just given, you are able to put your bucket down into the well again and draw some more.

11. Illustrate it! The use of illustrations is thoroughly biblical. Consider how much of Scripture is devoted to stories. Genesis to Job is almost entirely taken up with detailed accounts of battles fought, journeys taken, family quarrels, love stories and the accounts of supernatural signs and wonders. From Psalms to Malachi there are hundreds of poetic or prophetic pictures beautifully painted for us. In the New Testament, Matthew's Gospel through to the Acts of the Apostles is mostly in the narrative. Even in Paul's epistles he uses such metaphors as warfare, armour, building, body, fruit and farming. Finally, the Bible ends with a magnificent unfolding apocalyptic drama in the book of Revelation. Chapter by chapter the curtains are drawn back on scenes that are both awesome and breathtaking. If the use of illustrations is good enough for God, it ought to be good enough for us.

Some may wonder why all this is necessary. The plain reason is there are too many boring, inaccurate, lifeless, lacking in content and often irrelevant sermons being unloaded on God's poor longsuffering sheep. It doesn't take much intelligence to understand why so many church buildings are half empty on a Sunday morning and why people are becoming bored with what is being served up in home groups. With that I rest my case.

Spurgeon, regarded by many as the prince of preachers, gave the following seven reasons why preachers need to use anecdotes in their sermons:

(a) To interest the mind and secure the attention of the hearers. He said, 'We cannot endure a sleepy audience. To us a slumbering man is no man.' He goes on to mention a man called Hodge the hedger and ditcher, who once remarked, 'I loikes Sunday, I does; I loikes Sunday.' 'And what makes you like Sunday?' his companion asked. 'Because, you see, it's a day of rest; I goes down to the old church, I gets into a pew, and puts my feet up, and I thinks o' nothin'.'

(b) They render our preaching lifelike and vivid. George Whitefield liked to use illustrations in his sermons. On one occasion he was telling a story of a blind man with his dog walking on the edge of a precipice and his foot nearly slipping over the brink. Whitefield's graphic account was so vivid and lifelike that a certain Lord Chesterfield got entirely carried away and shot to his feet shouting, 'Good God! He's gone!' To which Whitefield responded, 'No, my Lord, he is not quite gone; let us hope he may yet be saved.'

(c) To explain either doctrines or duties to those of dull understanding. David Sheppard, one-time England cricketer and now the Anglican Bishop of Liverpool, was speaking on 'For all have sinned and come short of the glory of God' (Rom 3:23). He gave an arresting illustration of a test match in which he was narrowly stumped out by the wicket-keeper. It could only have been by a whisker, but 'out' he was! In another test match he strode down the pitch to meet the bowler, missed the ball entirely and was out by 6 or 7 feet. Both times he was declared 'out'; each time he came short. It could not have been put more clearly.

(d) There is a kind of reasoning in anecdotes and illustrations which is very clear to illogical minds. Spurgeon points out, 'Truthful anecdotes are facts, and facts are stubborn things.' When talking about God's awesome power in creation I like to mention that astronomers claim to have counted, thus far, 100 billion billion stars, as well as 100 billion galaxies. They say our own local galaxy has 1 trillion moons, of which we have visited one. The psalmist said, 'The heavens declare the glory of God.' Information like this is very difficult to shake off by those with illogical minds.

(e) They help the memory to grasp the truth. I was raised in a Christian home, so, in the past fifty-five years, I have heard several thousand sermons. The ones that have been retained in my memory are those that were amply illustrated.

(f) They frequently arouse the feelings. I love stories about Billy Bray or Evan Roberts and the Welsh revival. The Scottish Covenanters also have a special place in my heart. I have visited the martyrs' memorial site at Wigton, where Margaret Wilson was drowned at the hands of the wicked Claverhouse for her resolute faith in her Saviour in refusing to deny that Christ was the Head of the church. I stood over her grave and with tears thanked God for such heroes of the faith. There undoubtedly is a danger of using stories manipulatively. One way of guarding against this is to ask the question: 'Does the heart of the story perfectly match up with the spirit of the point being made?'

(g) They catch the ear of the utterly careless. People come into our meetings with all manner of thoughts grabbing their attention, especially mothers with young children or business men. They don't mean to be inattentive but their lives are so demanding. A suitable illustration will nicely catch their interest, and now their taste buds have been suitably stimulated they will more readily receive the rest of what you plan to shovel down their throats!

One final word about the use of illustrations. They are meant to be windows through which the hearer can see and gain a better grasp of the point you are endeavouring to communicate. They are not meant to be the point itself.

12. Apply it! Careful consideration needs to be given to the accurate interpretation of the Scriptures used and then the question needs to be asked; 'How does this apply to us today?' For example, Jesus told his disciples to wash each other's feet. As a matter of fact, I have had my feet washed by another believer, but not in a Western country, it was in the Middle East. It seems to me that a modern application of this Gospel account in a Western context would be for me to wash your car in the same way that Campbell McAlpine washed mine, a story I referred to earlier in this book. Thought also needs to be given in assessing your audience to make sure your application is relevant to their situation. What is the average age, are they working class, blue-collar workers or professional business class?

13. Take-off and landing! Every message needs a good introduction and a concise conclusion. I've heard many a preacher spoil a good sermon because he did not give enough care to get the message airborne or, having discharged his soul, he continued to encircle the airport or repeatedly made approaches to bring the sermon in to land only to abort the landing at the last moment. A suitable personal anecdote has a captivating way of catching the attention of your hearers and thus getting the plane off the ground. But then we need to safely land the thing. All preaching should be in faith. If it is in faith, then you are hoping for something to happen as a result of your ministry. If you have been giving a teaching to edify the saints then you could conclude with prayer asking the Lord to strengthen their hearts in the knowledge and love of God. If the message was dealing with forgiveness and reconciliation then a final exhortation for people to be obedient to the commands of Jesus may be appropriate. If it was on healing then an opportunity for people to be prayed for would be a natural conclusion. Of course, all of these suggestions would be subject to you being guided by the Holy Spirit. But as much care and consideration needs to be given to the ending as was given to the main heart of the message.

14. Don't overspiritualise the parables! Down through the history of the church, preachers have tended to read more into a parable than was intended. For example, Saint Augustine, when explaining the story of the man who was robbed on the road from Jerusalem to Jericho, interpreted the four legs of the donkey to represent the four Gospels! How he arrived at that conclusion only the good saint knows. Jesus was usually making one point which was often mentioned before he commenced the parable.

15. Be consistent! Keep constant with your rules of interpretation when handling books like Ezekiel and Revelation. Without getting too embroiled on this point, let's take one example. If the picture being painted isn't real but rather represents something which is real, then we must stay with that method throughout the book. If a star is an angel, if a candlestick is a church, and the waters referred to in Revelation 17:15 are peoples, multitudes, nations and tongues, then 144,000 cannot literally mean that number, nor 1,000 years be a literal 1,000 years.

16. Look for the real meaning! Look for lessons rather than hidden meanings. Having been raised in a denomination that placed great value on excessive use of types and shadows, I can easily understand how they were able to take all the miracles and apply them spiritually. The blind became spiritually blind, the lame spiritually lame, so we never anointed the sick with oil and prayed for them, even though there are explicit instructions to do so in James 5:14. Now to be fair, I have a number of very close friends who have strong positive convictions regarding the use of types and shadows and who move powerfully in praying for the sick. My feelings are simply this: that while the Holy Spirit was pleased to take Old Testament situations and events and use them allegorically in the New Testament, this does not give me the authority to make up my own and do it myself. My job is to expound what is already there, not add to it.

17. Never plagiarise! If you use other people's material make sure you always give the credit to the author of preacher. It is part of the preacher's integrity. Of course, the older you get the more you accumulate facts, figures, ideas and insights which become so much a part of you and your ministry that you lose track of where it all originated from. However, whenever it's possible, it's nice to mention the source. It encourages people to trust you.

18. Be careful of secular sources! Never use a secular dictionary to explain Bible words. If you find yourself questioning this advice, please take the time to look up the word 'love' in *Vine's Expository Dictionary* and compare it with *Chambers Dictionary* or *The Oxford Dictionary*. There is no similarity.

19. Avoid prejudice! Don't be over-enamoured with any one particular commentary, or any one particular theologian. It is amazing how completely opposite they can be with their strongly held positions. If the so-called experts disagree on such matters as the Second Coming of our Lord, eternal security, eternal punishment and a host of other Bible subjects, then we should be careful not to put our confidence in one single source, but draw from a wide range of scholars and, of course, the Holy Spirit whom Jesus promised would guide us into all truth.

20. Try to improve your diction! Mumbling, excessive 'ums' and 'ahs', running words together and failing to sound the ends of your words all combine to make your preaching difficult to listen to. Avoid talking in a monotone. Talking with an affected parsonic voice and using religious platitudes are the preacher's unpardonable sins—nothing drives away the unchurched faster. I'm a bit of a sinner myself when it comes to the use of 'ums' and 'ahs'; I am particularly bad when I'm nervous. The more conversant I am with my subject the more comfortable I am with its delivery. As to pronouncing the ends of my words, that was greatly improved by practising when singing hymns.

21. Practise eye contact! When preaching keep good eye contact with the congregation. There is not much worse than having a preacher speak to the back wall or the air duct. In a small group situation I like to draw people into the talk by name as if I was having a personal conversation with them.

22. Kiss (which according to Corrie ten Boom stands for 'Keep it simple, stupid!') is an ideal exhortation to all communicators! Billy Graham says he aims his message at fourteen-year-olds in the 'B' stream. I think we can all agree he's been very successful with that assessment.

Big words fail to impress anybody. Our use of them is usually a sign of insecurity. The New Testament was written in the common language of ordinary people; our preaching should imitate it.

23. Stand up! Speak up! and Shut up! We are too long-winded, especially in house groups or small congregations. Twenty-five to forty minutes is sufficient time to say all that needs to be said at one sitting.

24. Don't be afraid of theological terminology! It won't bite you!

(a) *Exegesis* means finding out what it really says.

(b) *Hermeneutics* means interpreting and applying what it really says.

(c) *Homiletics* means presenting what it really says.

Finally! I want to put in a plea for the restoration of good old-fashioned expository Bible teaching. It is hardly ever used among the new churches, resulting in gaping holes in the biblical understanding of many. Without teaching a whole book at a time we are almost certain to miss out important basic doctrines of the faith. You might ask yourself the question: 'When last did you give or hear a teaching on the Second Coming of Christ?'

I have been carrying out a test as I have travelled around various churches by asking the question: 'When last did you hear a sermon on the Second Coming?' The usual response out of a congregation of 150 is that two or three have heard one in the last two years, a further thirty, during the past ten years, but the majority have never heard one.

Sad to say, there seem to exist too many three-string

theological guitars! An essential part of a leader's responsibility is to feed God's sheep on knowledge and understanding. We must endeavour to teach the whole counsel
of God.

Enjoy your preaching. Remember! Good seed will
always produce good fruit.

19

Murphy Versus O'Shaunessy:
When Calamity Strikes

Murphy's law simply speaking is: 'Everything that can go wrong will go wrong.' O'Shaunessy is of the opinion that things are generally much worse, so his law is: 'Murphy is an optimist.'

A leader needs to be prepared at all times to handle every type of calamity. During my twenty-seven years as a pastor I have conducted numerous weddings. I have discovered they rarely go entirely to plan. I have watched nervously as a bridegroom, reciting his vows, began to turn ashen white—I could see him gradually slipping away into a state of unconsciousness as he slowly swayed from side to side. Finally, just in the nick of time, I managed to grab hold of him before he collapsed to the ground.

I have watched a bride become faint as she struggled to say her vows and then throw up into the hands of the bridegroom—as gallant a young man as I have ever met!

I have waited an hour and a half for the bride to arrive as I mentioned in a previous chapter—she was trapped in the middle of a carnival procession.

On another occasion, the bride was delayed forty-five minutes because one of the page boys during a pre-service photo session in the bride's back garden had fallen into the pond. His beautiful white satin shirt and velvet trousers were smothered in thick green slime. How his mother washed, dried and then pressed those clothes and was only forty-five minutes late I will never know!

At one wedding I attended, the pastor officiating asked the question: 'Who gives this man to be married to this woman?' Who indeed? In another wedding I asked the bride's father, 'Who gives this woman to be married to this man?' He replied, 'Your mother and I do.' My mother didn't even know the couple and was about 5,000 miles away at the time.

However, those were all minor catastrophes compared with the one that occurred during a wedding that my good friend Michael was conducting. It happened to be his first wedding so he was naturally feeling rather nervous.

The ceremony was proceeding quite smoothly. It was a beautiful day, ideal for a wedding. The church building was packed with guests, all smartly turned out, many of whom had travelled a long distance to be there. All progressed well until Michael asked the groom, 'Will you take this woman to be your lawful wedded wife?' The response was a stony silence. Michael, thinking the groom might not have heard the question clearly, repeated it, only this time more emphatically: 'Will you take this woman to be your lawful wedded wife?' Again there was no reply. You could feel the tension rising. Michael by now was getting a little flustered, and leaning forward in a loud stage-whisper he instructed the groom to say, 'I will.' 'I know,' said the groom, 'but I'm not sure I'm doing the right thing.' At this point the bride began to sob uncontrollably. 'Please say it honey,' she pleaded, but all to no avail. He could only look at her in dismay and respond, 'I'm sorry sweetheart, I can't.'

By this time Michael could see he had a full-scale disaster on his hands. He knew he couldn't deal with it in front of the astonished congregation, so he hurriedly ushered the bridal party into the vestry. They were quickly followed by the now extremely distressed and bewildered parents.

After some fifteen minutes of agonising discussion Michael finally returned to the stunned congregation and informed them that the wedding was off! However, they were all welcome to attend the wedding banquet, if they so desired. For those who attended it must have been more like a funeral wake than a reception.

Michael's next wedding was almost as bad as the first. This time the ceremony was held in a beautiful, terraced garden, in idyllic surroundings—the perfect setting for such a special occasion. The backdrop to the bridal party was an open valley. Behind them was a low, 1-foot-high wall, then a 6-foot drop to the next tier.

All was proceeding well until the bride handed her bouquet to the chief bridesmaid for the exchanging of the rings. As she stepped back, having received the bouquet, she went a little too far and tripped over the wall, falling headlong onto a path 6 feet beneath. The result was a severely lacerated head and a fractured skull. Pandemonium broke out as women guests screamed and children cried. The bride herself leapt over the wall in an attempt to help but in so doing sprained her ankle. Blood soaked into her lovely white wedding dress as she knelt beside her best friend. A short while later, an ambulance arrived and conveyed the poor unfortunate bridesmaid to hospital.

Michael quickly concluded the ceremony and spent the rest of his time consoling the bride and the couple's family.

Funerals

Unfortunately, Murphy and O'Shaunessy often attend funerals. Is nothing sacred? I have heard of the grave not being large enough to receive the coffin, the hearse ending up in a ditch after having a collision with another vehicle on an icy road, not to mention punctured tyres, roadworks and level-crossing gates which were shut.

It is most important to discover in which cemetery the deceased is going to be interred. Stephen, a Baptist pastor, had concluded the main part of the funeral service in the chapel. Now all that remained was the burial at the cemetery. He normally travelled in the hearse with the coffin but on this occasion he needed a quick getaway after the committal, so he travelled in his own car. Unfortunately he assumed wrongly that the burial was at the main cemetery. It didn't take too long for him to discover his 'grave' mistake. Panic gripped hold of him as he realised that it could be any one of four other places! Driving as if he was at Le Mans, he pulled up with screeching tyres at the next possible location. Fortunately it was the right one. The funeral cortege was just drawing up to the gates!

Funerals are naturally solemn occasions but sometimes, as happened to another minister friend of mine, things occur that make it difficult to keep a straight face. He had just announced the opening hymn which was number 412 in the hymnbook. Immediately someone at the back called out emotionally, 'That was her Co-op number!' Several workmates attended Charlie's funeral at the crematorium. As the conveyor shuttled the coffin out of sight, one of them shouted, 'Goodbye Charlie!'

I think my friend Michael of wedding fame is a bit of a Jonah. The first funeral he took was as bad as his first wedding. It was at the time of the troubles in Zimbabwe, in fact the deceased had been murdered by a terrorist group.

The service was at the crematorium. The custom was for the coffin to be already placed in the chapel before the mourners arrived. Everyone was gathering outside waiting for the procession into the chapel to begin. Finally all were present, so Michael opened the door and commenced to lead them down the aisle, reciting suitable portions of Scripture as he went. Halfway down it dawned on him that there was no coffin present. He broke out into a cold sweat. What to do? He couldn't continue as things were, so finally he turned around and said, 'Folks, I'm afraid there has been a mistake—there's no coffin.' There was a dreadful silence, then suddenly in the distance he could hear the high revs of an engine and the screeching of brakes. They all hurried back to the entrance to be met by a very embarrassed undertaker, who apologised profusely explaining that the police had refused to release the body because their murder inquiry was incomplete!

The key to handling Murphy and O'Shaunessy situations is first of all, don't panic. It's not a matter of life and death. (Most of the incidents will make wonderful anecdotes for preaching material later on. . . .)

Second, lighten up a little; we all tend to take ourselves far too seriously. Learn how to turn the mistakes into an opportunity for people to have a laugh at your expense. Some people get paid large sums of money to make people laugh at their staged misfortune. It certainly helps to keep them awake.

Third, try to cash in on unexpected mishaps. On one occasion I was the invited speaker for the annual meeting of a certain national youth organisation. I was at Bible school at the time and this was my first big public speaking engagement. I was anxious to make a good impression. I noticed from the programme that I was to speak for twenty minutes following a 'Fact and Faith' film. Now for anyone who may not realise it, speaking after a film has been shown is even worse than having to speak immediately after lunch. Sure enough, it was as bad as I expected—the young people were lounging around all bleary-eyed and obviously uninterested in listening to this total stranger. Shortly after commencing to speak, I took a step back. Unfortunately my heel caught the leg of a chair and down I went, dumped unceremoniously on my back. The whole hall erupted into laughter and while I struggled to regain my composure it dawned on me that I had their undivided attention.

That night quite a number of young people gave their lives to Christ and I learned a valuable lesson: treat mistakes as if they are a friend and not an enemy, use them as a blessing and not a curse. Even if it was Satan himself who was behind the calamity, God can turn it for good if we are willing to be fools for Christ's sake.

20

Things to Do or Not to Do

In this closing chapter there are twenty important things to which the pastor needs to give special attention. Failure to do so could seriously undermine his ministry.

1. Always guard the spiritual environment of that which has been entrusted to you by God. It is so easy for a house group to develop into a social club. On one occasion under my own pastoral leadership, I was shocked to discover that one house group had not opened a Bible for over six months!

Never tolerate the existence of gossip. We are told in Proverbs 17:9 that it separates intimate friends. Nothing will destroy the spiritual environment of a community faster than the toleration of idle talk.

Make sure that broken relationships are resolved, especially at leadership level. If reconciliation is not forthcoming, it is not long before people begin to take sides and a party spirit is established.

2. Never relocate a problem to solve it otherwise you will end up compounding it. A person with a wounded spirit will continue to react anywhere and everywhere. An individual who operates out of insecurity or rejection won't improve because of a change of location. The problem lies within; only through embracing the cross will freedom ultimately be experienced.

3. Be patient when counselling people with deep-seated problems; don't expect miracles from one session. It is usually helpful to give assignments in order to help form new behaviour patterns. Deliverance may get rid of demons but it doesn't remove the original cause of the demons getting there. Memory strongholds are often established which are not easily disposed of. In fact, they consist of actual chemical substances in the brain. Patience and gentleness is the only way to handle God's sick or injured sheep.

It is important that we remember how graciously the Lord has handled us over the years and how he still continues to extend his mercies toward us.

4. Without becoming paranoid, take care not to explain away the inner disquiet regarding the spiritual condition of those in your care. Paul encourages the elders from Ephesus in Acts 20:28: 'Be on guard for yourselves and for all the flock, among which the Holy Spirit has made you overseers.'

Legalism is often a cover for sexual sin. The more insistent, the worse the sin. Take note when people go out of their way to avoid eye contact.

Excessive busy-ness can be another indication that all is not well.

A critical spirit is often a clue of the existence of serious trouble. Proverbs 18:1 points out: 'He who separates himself seeks his own desire, he quarrels against all sound wisdom.'

5. Never be expedient in the appointment of new leaders. Paul instructs Timothy in 1 Timothy 5:22: 'Do not lay hands upon anyone too hastily and thus share responsibility for the sins of others.'

If a potential leader behaves passively in the meetings by not praying, exercising the gifts or by not raising hands in worship, then that person ought not to be considered for eldership. Too many times when visiting churches I've noticed elders standing silent in times of worship with their hands in their pockets, gazing around totally uninvolved with everyone else. Such men ought not to remain as elders if they are not willing to give a lead.

6. Refrain at all times from using an occasion when you minister as an opportunity to either defend yourself or attack your critics. Whenever a pastor indulges in such foolishness he always loses a measure of the congregation's confidence and respect in his leadership.

7. Avoid sharp U-turns; they cause the insecure to panic. Careful preparation of the people before change is thrust upon them is always helpful. If it happens to be a major new direction, the older saints especially appreciate being consulted before the matter comes before the rest of the church.

8. Very rarely will one sermon make such an impact that it radically changes the church. Vernon Simpson, father of Charles Simpson who is mentioned elsewhere in this book, once counselled his son when he was a young pastor, 'Son, if you sow the right seed you will harvest the right fruit.' My experience is that it takes weeks, if not months, of carefully sowing the seed until faith rises in the people and before change can take place without serious upheaval. I felt the Lord impress upon me in my early days as a pastor, 'Keep the kettle on the boil.'

One message once a year on Pentecost Sunday dealing with the subject of being filled with the Holy Spirit will never get people exercising the gifts of the Spirit nor change the church into becoming charismatic.

9. Never run away from the problems, or wait, hoping they will go away of their own accord. Nothing wears a pastor out faster than unresolved problems. It is not being suggested that hasty, prayerless, ill-conceived solutions are the answer; but it is a warning that difficult situations swept under the carpet will only return to create a much worse situation.

One of the keys to successful leadership is to be a good problem-solver. The tendency is to deal with little problems first before tackling the more serious ones, but it never works! Give your emotional and spiritual energy to the big ones first and just occasionally you might be pleasantly surprised to discover that some of the little ones take care of themselves.

10. Let your words always have integrity. Exaggeration will seriously undermine your effectiveness as a leader. It is a shame to listen to people say of their pastors that they need generally to reduce his claims of numbers by 50 per cent; or that he always speaks evangelistically! It is difficult to trust someone who isn't honest with his words. In James 3:2 we read: 'If anyone does not stumble in what he says, he is a perfect man, able to bridle the whole body as well.' Put another way, James could well be implying if I cannot control my tongue then it is likely that I won't be able to control the rest of my body. That sounds pretty serious.

11. If delegating responsibilities to others is good enough for God, it ought to be good enough for us. If we want to retain a 'one-man' ministry system as opposed to a body ministry then we should never delegate.

If we want to keep those whom God has entrusted to our care in perpetual childhood, then we should never delegate any authority to them.

If we want to have a nervous breakdown or go to an

early grave, then whatever we do we must make sure we do most of it, if not all of it, ourselves!

12. Diffident, indecisive leadership of meetings is a killer. It is one thing genuinely to wait for the leading of the Spirit, but quite another to be ill-prepared.

Ian Bilby, an Elim pastor from Auckland, New Zealand, regularly has sessions with his leaders where they ask the question: 'What are we doing in our meetings that scatters people and what are we doing that gathers them?'

13. William Law, writing in the eighteenth century, said, 'Man needs to be saved from his own wisdom as much as he needs to be saved from his own righteousness, for they produce the same corruption.' Eating from the tree of knowledge of good and evil is strictly forbidden by God. It was an offence so heinous that God had to evict Adam and Eve from the Garden of Eden.

God's indictment of Israel in Jerusalem 7:24 was, 'They...walked in their own counsels.' Also, in Jeremiah 2:13 God says, 'For My people have committed two evils: they have forsaken Me, the fountain of living waters, to hew for themselves cisterns; broken cisterns, that can hold no water.'

In Proverbs 3:5–7 we read: 'Trust in the Lord with all your heart, and do not lean on your own understanding. In all your ways acknowledge Him, and He will make your paths straight. Do not be wise in your own eyes.'

Some years ago, whilst pastoring in the Baptist Church, Basingstoke, a lady approached me asking for urgent help. She was suffering from deep depression which was clearly evident in her countenance. She was a medical doctor, an East Indian, and a Christian. I invited her to tell her story, which turned out to have a direct bearing on the cause of her trouble.

It happened that she met and fell in love with another doctor, also an East Indian, but a Hindu. As the relationship deepened, she realised that unless he became a Christian, she would be unable to marry him. So she talked him into becoming a nominal Christian, taking him to Kingsway Methodist Church in London, where he went through a formal public demonstration of becoming a Christian by being christened. The reality was that it was a conversion of convenience.

They were soon married but almost immediately she began to feel periods of intense guilt. Gradually, an overwhelming darkness seemed to envelop her soul, until she found herself only managing to sleep for brief moments at a time. She became intensely obsessed with the idea that she had committed the unpardonable sin, so she had come to me as a final resort.

First, I asked her whether she had confessed her sin to Jesus, assuring her that 'If we confess our sin he is faithful and just to forgive us our sin and cleanse us from all unrighteousness.' She responded that she had indeed confessed her sin but it had made no difference. I felt helpless. All I could do was to point out further scriptures that dealt with sin, confession and forgiveness, at the same time recommending that she commit them to memory and meditate on them every time she felt the depression intensifying.

Then I had a bright idea that I had used once before. I asked her whether she had in fact received Christ's forgiveness. This seemed to strike a chord. She hadn't done so as far as she could remember but was willing to do it immediately. With great sincerity she told the Lord she received his forgiveness, closing her prayer by thanking him for all his wonderful grace and mercy. As I showed her to the door I felt full of confidence that she had turned a corner and that we could expect to see a full recovery.

A few days later, to my dismay, I learned that her condition had deteriorated even further. Shortly afterwards, following a Sunday evening service, I saw her being led by the arm in my direction and my heart sank. I ushered her with her friend into the vestry. The friend explained that the next day the doctor was being admitted to the local mental hospital for electric shock treatment. This was the same hospital where her husband was a consultant psychiatrist. Could I pray for her further to see if God might intervene? I again resorted to the Bible verses that had been shared with her previously but once again there was no success. All the time I failed to realise that I had been eating of the tree of knowledge of good and evil instead of going to the Tree of Life, the Lord Jesus.

Suddenly it dawned on me what I had been doing. I requested that we had a time of silent prayer, during which I sent up one of the most urgent SOS prayers I have ever prayed: 'Lord, forgive me for behaving independently; I've been leaning to my own understanding. For the sake of this poor lady have mercy both on her and myself.' Immediately into my thoughts came the phrase 'James 5'. I thought, 'How can it be James chapter 5, that has to do with being healed from sickness?' Again came the phrase 'James 5'. I still continued to reason why it should be healing when the issue was guilt. If I had taken the trouble to look up the Scripture I would have noticed the sentence, 'And if he has committed sins, they will be forgiven him.'

Once more the words 'James 5' came to my mind. I turned to the doctor and said, 'Sister, do you believe that Jesus heals the sick?' Her answer, without a word spoken, was to get off her seat and kneel on the floor. The presence of God filled that little vestry—it was awesome.

Filled with faith, I laid hands on her head and prayed for her healing. The only way I can explain it is that I knew because I knew that God was healing her right there and then. She rose from the floor, her face radiant, the glazed listless eyes were now sparkling with joy. It all happened in less than two minutes.

My good ideas had failed miserably and had taken up

weeks of unnecessary suffering. Two minutes of eating from the Tree of Life and the result was—a miracle.

The story doesn't end there, for when she got home her husband met her at the door and was absolutely astounded with the dramatic change in the countenance of his wife. A few days later he genuinely gave his life to Jesus and received him as Lord and Saviour.

14. Praying for the sick and casting out demons should be the normal ministry of the caring pastor. In Matthew 9:36 we read of Jesus: 'Seeing the multitudes, He felt compassion for them, because they were distressed [harassed] and downcast [thrown down] like sheep without a shepherd.' Jesus then exhorts his disciples to pray that the Lord of the harvest would send out workers into his harvest. The story continues on into chapter 10. Bearing in mind that there were no chapter and verse divisions in the original text, we find Jesus commissioning the Twelve and giving them authority over unclean spirits, to cast them out, and to heal every kind of disease and every kind of sickness.

I am writing this chapter in Zululand, South Africa, in the home of a Zulu pastor. He has just told me how he prayed for the wife of the chief who lives next door and she was wonderfully healed of continuous menstrual bleeding similar to the case of the ministry of Jesus. As a result he was able to share the gospel with her and she gave her life to Christ. Eventually the chief's three other wives also trusted in Christ. Last Sunday the chief (who is also a government minister) asked the pastor if he would come and pray a blessing on him as he was about to visit the United States on government business.

Praying for the sick is part of the pastor's portfolio; failure to do so is an abrogation of his responsibility.

15. Always ensure that the saints entrusted to your care receive good quality teaching, full of biblical content.

I heard someone say on one occasion, 'If we take care of the depth of our ministry, God will take care of the breadth.' We in the new churches have had a tendency to be strong in the exhorting and prophetic style of ministry, which can frequently be inordinately subjective and rather weak in the teaching gift. My observation over the years is that too much exhortation wears out the saints.

Exhortation does not necessarily bring refreshment to a person's spirit; on the contrary, it can often bring a sense of condemnation. Greater care needs to be taken to make sure a healthy diet is being served. Anointing should never be a replacement for shallow preparation.

16. The measure and importance of prayer in a church determines its spiritual health and effectiveness. Every church that majors in prayer will be successful in making an impact in its locality. It may not have the largest congregation but its influence will greatly exceed that of larger fellowships which place less of a priority on prayer.

It is the elders' responsibility to encourage and facilitate the prayer life of the community. Ideally, someone who is a mature intercessor ought to have the government of leading the prayer life of the church. This doesn't have to be the pastor; he has usually got far too many things on his mind to give prayer the necessary attention it deserves. Naturally the pastor needs to be enthusiastically involved, but someone who can devote their time and energy exclusively to stimulating prayer and keeping it high on the agenda can only be a great asset. Nights or half nights of prayer, days of prayer and fasting, early morning prayer meetings, ladies prayer groups, prayer triplets, prayer chains and, more recently, concerts of prayer, are all ways in which God's people can give themselves effectively to the grand and holy task of prayer.

17. Anointed praise and worship is also essential to the healthy growth of the church. Wherever there is quality praise and worship, people are drawn to such meetings. I believe one of the reasons is that it touches the eternal in the human spirit. It connects with the internal sense that tells us we were born for the purpose of worshipping God. Jesus told us that the Father seeks for those who will worship him in spirit and in truth. Music is one of God's precious gifts to mankind. What could be more fulfilling than to join with other believers around the throne of God and of the Lamb accompanied by a variety of musical instruments and to blend our voices together in worship of him who is worthy to receive power and riches and wisdom and might and honour and glory and blessing?

The fact that in recent years there has been a dramatic increase in the sale of worship tapes is clear evidence that there was a thirst in the hearts of God's people that needed to be satisfied.

18. We should never be ambiguous about our vision. If we don't have one, we need to seek the face of God until we get one. If we only see it vaguely, then we will doubtless communicate it vaguely.

There should not only be a vision for the church as a whole but there should be one for each department. For instance, I look at it this way.

(a) What is my vision for prayer in the church?
Who is responsible for it?
Who do I see in charge of it five years from now?
What am I doing about preparing that person now?

(b) What is my vision for evangelism?
Who is responsible for it now?
Who do I see in charge of it five years from now?
What am I doing about preparing that person now?

The same questions need to be asked regarding the prophetic life of the church, the children, the young people, the senior citizens, the women, teaching, pastoral care, praise and worship, plus all the other activities of the fellowship.

19. Avoid at all costs the male propensity for abstract theorising of irrelevant theological issues. It's a killer! Far too much time is wasted in elders' meetings on doubts and theories, instead of getting on with prayer and dealing with pertinent matters. The pastor needs to be decisive and to keep the discussion geared to action.

I feel sorry for some of those poor souls who annually attend the big Bible week conventions. They get filled with mighty visions, but because there is no opportunity for these visions to be practically fulfilled back home in their local church, all they are left with after a few months is some exciting memories. It is possible that attendance at a Bible week could be an inoculation against the real thing. The Bible week conventions are not to blame; the fault lies with church leaders who, as Bob Mumford puts it, 'are like stewards on the *Titanic* rearranging the deckchairs while the ship goes under'. In other words, the elders are majoring in minors.

20. We now come to the last on my list, which is the most important of all. The pastor should take painstaking care to foster a tender, sensitive spirit toward the Lord.

It is all too easy to develop a hard heart. We need continually to pray, 'Melt my heart, O Lord, keep it ever true.' The Scriptures tell us that God will not despise a broken and a contrite heart, and in Isaiah 66:2 we read, 'But to this one I will look, to him who is humble and contrite of spirit, and who trembles at My word.'

One of the cherished memories I have of the late Arthur Wallis was being present with him at a prayer retreat during which someone started to sing, 'Just as I am, without one plea, but that they blood was shed for me, and that thou bid'st me come to thee, O Lamb of God, I come.' As the remaining verses were being sung,

Arthur lay prostrate on his face before the Lord, weeping like a child. A soft tender heart toward God is the one thing I think I desire more than anything else.

Reading devotional books by authors such as E.W. Tozer and other books that tell of God's special visitations in times of revival, all helps to create and maintain a thirst in my soul for the living God.

May God raise up leaders in our nation who have a Holy Spirit-inspired passion for the Person of Christ. And may you and I be among them.

Epilogue

Thank you for taking the trouble to read this book to the end. As I said in the Preface, these chapters are not meant to be a treatise on pastoral care, but are lessons and principles that have been built into my pastoral ministry through mistakes, pain and disappointment as well as wise counsel from choice men of God.

I do not claim to have apprehended all the principles necessary to make an effective pastor. In fact, I frequently feel woefully inadequate, but by God's grace I press on, seeking to attain to become the type of pastor God speaks of in Jeremiah 3:15: 'Then I will give you shepherds after My own heart, who will feed you on knowledge and understanding.' And again in Jeremiah 23:4: 'I shall also raise up shepherds over them and they will tend them; and they will not be afraid any longer, nor be terrified, nor will any be missing.'